The Elements of Wood Ship Construction

William Henry Curtis

THE ELEMENTS OF
WOOD SHIP CONSTRUCTION

McGraw-Hill Book Co. Inc.

PUBLISHERS OF BOOKS FOR

Coal Age ▽ Electric Railway Journal
Electrical World ▽ Engineering News-Record
American Machinist ▽ The Contractor
Engineering & Mining Journal ▽ Power
Metallurgical & Chemical Engineering
Electrical Merchandising

THE ELEMENTS

OF

WOOD SHIP CONSTRUCTION

BY

W. H. CURTIS
NAVAL ARCHITECT AND MARINE ENGINEER

FIRST EDITION

McGRAW-HILL BOOK COMPANY, Inc.
239 WEST 39TH STREET. NEW YORK

LONDON: HILL PUBLISHING CO., Ltd.
6 & 8 BOUVERIE ST., E. C.

1919

THE MAPLE PRESS YORK PA

GENERAL PREFACE

Preface to Pamphlet, Part I, issued by the United States Shipping Board Emergency Fleet Corporation, for use in its classes in Wood Shipbuilding.

This text on wood shipbuilding was prepared by W. H. Curtis, Portland, Oregon, for the Education and Training Section of the Emergency Fleet Corporation. It is intended for the use of carpenters and others, who, though skilled in their work, lack the detail knowledge of ships necessary for the efficient performance of their work in the yard.

Sea-going vessels are generally built according to the rules of some Classification Society, and all important construction and fastening details have to be passed upon by the Classification Society under whose inspection the vessel is to be built. Due to this fact, requirements may vary in detail from types of construction here explained. It is hoped, however, that this book may be helpful to shipbuilding classes and to individual men in the yard.

EDUCATION AND TRAINING SECTION

**UNITED STATES SHIPPING BOARD
EMERGENCY FLEET CORPORATION**

In presenting this work due credit is given Mr. L. G. Nichols, Director of Education of the Portland, Oregon, Y. M. C. A., not only for his active encouragement which led to the compiling of these chapters in book form, but also for his energetic progressiveness in organizing the first successful class in wood shipbuilding in the United States, the conducting of which necessitated the collecting of most of the information contained herein.

For purposes of publication the subject matter as presented to this class has been completely revised and enlarged, and while it is realized that it still falls short of presenting every detail of the ship, it is hoped that the subject has been sufficiently covered to afford a valuable guide and aid to workmen and students.

W. H. CURTIS.

CONTENTS

ELEMENTS OF

WOOD SHIP CONSTRUCTION

CHAPTER I

KEELS, STEMS AND STERN POSTS

KEEL BLOCKS

"THE SHIP'S FOUNDATION"

Every structure must have a suitable foundation. Floating structures, such as ships, are built on temporary foundations called slips. When completed they are then launched, or permitted to slide into the water.

While the slip is purely a temporary foundation for the ship during construction, it usually is permanent in itself and may be used for many ships.

The slip usually consists of a very strong arrangement of piling, suitably capped, and decked over with heavy planks. The decking of the slip serves as a working platform under the ship. Since the ship must be launched into the water it is necessary for end launchings to build the slip on an incline which slopes downward toward the water. This slope is usually about $\frac{5}{8}$ to $\frac{3}{4}$ of an inch to the foot, *i. e.*, $\frac{5}{8}$ to $\frac{3}{4}$ of an inch of fall to one foot of length.

The keel blocks are arranged on top of the slip. They serve to carry the weight of the ship and to obtain the proper working room between the ship's bottom and the slip. Keel blocks must be so built as to be easily removed just before the ship is launched. The keel is the first piece in any ship to be assembled in the building slip, and since the keel blocks form the foundation proper for the keel, it is necessary to have them in place before the keel can be laid.

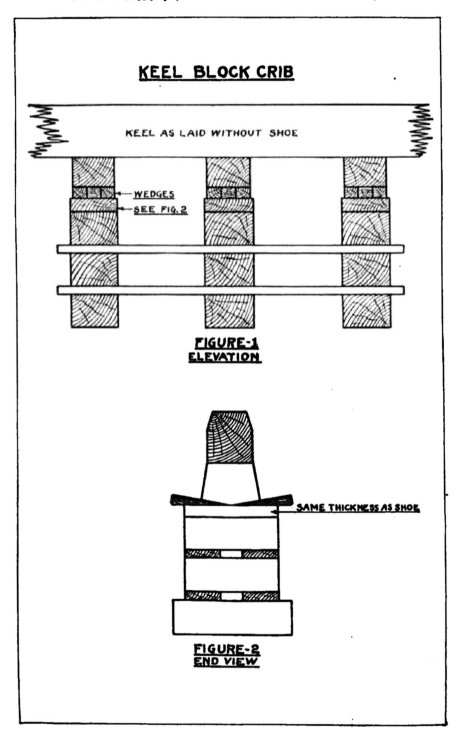

KEEL BLOCK CRIB

KEEL AS LAID WITHOUT SHOE

WEDGES

SEE FIG.2

FIGURE-1
ELEVATION

SAME THICKNESS AS SHOE

FIGURE-2
END VIEW

Keel blocks may be cribbed, as in Figs. 1 and 2, or plain, as in Figs. 3 and 4. The cribbing is to steady the blocks during the early part of construction, when they do not carry much weight. At least half of the blocks should be cribbed, and in some yards they are all cribbed. In all cases they must be placed directly over the piling of the slip. Thus the spacing of the keel blocks is regulated by the bents of piling under the slip. This is ordinarily six to eight feet from center to center of the blocks.

Since the slip has an incline, the keel blocks, if left square on the bottom, would not stand plumb, but would lean toward the lower end of the slip. If wide blocking is used, say 18 inches or over, this inclination of the blocks need not be considered. If the blocking is much narrower than 18 inches, the bottom block should be scribed off so that the entire set will stand plumb. Where the blocks are cribbed this latter operation involves a great deal of extra work on the upper and lower blocks, as the cribbing planks, if the block stands plumb, must stand on a level. It is, therefore, economy to use wide blocking and then permit the set to lean with the slip.

The top, or wedge, block should be shaped as shown in Fig. 3 and fitted with wedges to be used in lining up the keel. Good proportions and proper settings for wedges are shown in Figs. 5 and 6.

If a shoe or false keel is to be fitted it cannot be placed until the frames have been erected and the keelson is in place and fastened down, as the main keelson bolts are clinched up under the keel. Therefore, an extra block, having the same thickness as the shoe, should be fitted above the cribbing and under the wedge block, as shown in Figs. 1 and 2. This block is to be removed when the shoe is fitted, as shown in Fig. 3.

Keels are customarily laid on the same slope as the slip. However, since wood ships have considerable tendency to hog, *i. e.*, drop at the ends, after launching, the keel is laid with a spring, or sag, in the middle. Thus, when the vessel hogs slightly after launching, the keel, instead of

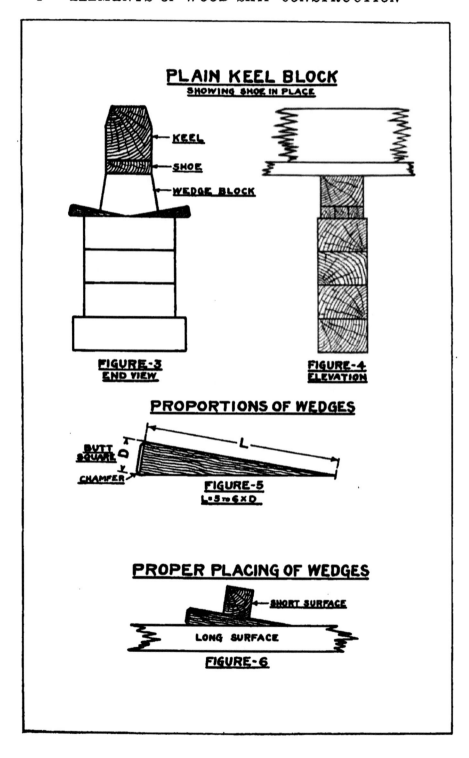

PLAIN KEEL BLOCK
SHOWING SHOE IN PLACE

KEEL

SHOE

WEDGE BLOCK

FIGURE-3
END VIEW

FIGURE-4
ELEVATION

PROPORTIONS OF WEDGES

BUTT
SQUARE
D
L
CHAMFER

FIGURE-5
L=5 TO 6 X D

PROPER PLACING OF WEDGES

SHORT SURFACE

LONG SURFACE

FIGURE-6

showing the hog, merely tends to straighten out. The amount of spring used varies greatly with different designers. A fair average would be between 1½ and 2 inches for each 100 feet of keel length.

Where the keel is laid on the same slope as the slip the two end blocks will be the same height. The middle block will be lower by just the amount of the spring. On the blocks between the middle and the ends the spring is roughly estimated when the blocks are first set up, the final adjustment being made by dubbing the top block, or driving and slackening the wedges after the keel is up. The tops of the wedge blocks must be dubbed to fay accurately to the bottom of the keel.

The blocks and cribs should not be spiked together. If it is necessary to steady the blocks while the keel is being laid, they should be lightly toenailed. The nails should be removed as soon as the blocks have enough weight on them to be steady.

The height of keel blocks used in different yards is by no means uniform. However, the distance from the top of the slipway planking to the top of the keel should not be less than five feet, nor more than six feet.

LAYING OUT THE KEEL

The first step in laying out the keel is to locate and scribe across the top and down each side all frame centers on each piece of the keel, as shown on the plans. These are then numbered in the same order as marked on the plans. This is very important, as nearly all construction details in ships are located by frame numbers. The frame center-lines should be scribed with a race knife, and the numbers marked with heavy blue or black crayon.

The plans show the location of the scarfs, and these may now be accurately marked out between the proper frames. The nibs of scarfs, unless otherwise called for, should land about half way between frame centers. If a scarf six depths long is too short to land thus, it should be made

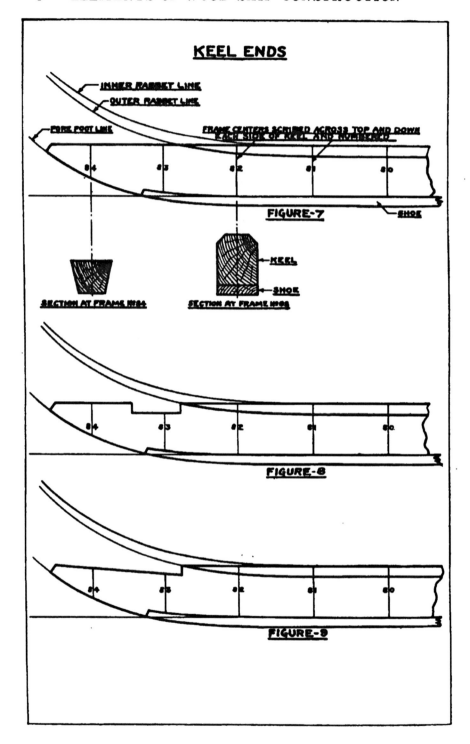

KEEL ENDS

INNER RABBET LINE

OUTER RABBET LINE

PORE FOOT LINE

FRAME CENTERS SCRIBED ACROSS TOP AND DOWN EACH SIDE OF KEEL AND NUMBERED

#4   #3   #2   #1   #0

FIGURE-7

SHOE

KEEL

SHOE

SECTION AT FRAME N=4   SECTION AT FRAME N=2

#4   #3   #2   #1   #0

FIGURE-8

#4   #3   #2   #1   #0

FIGURE-9

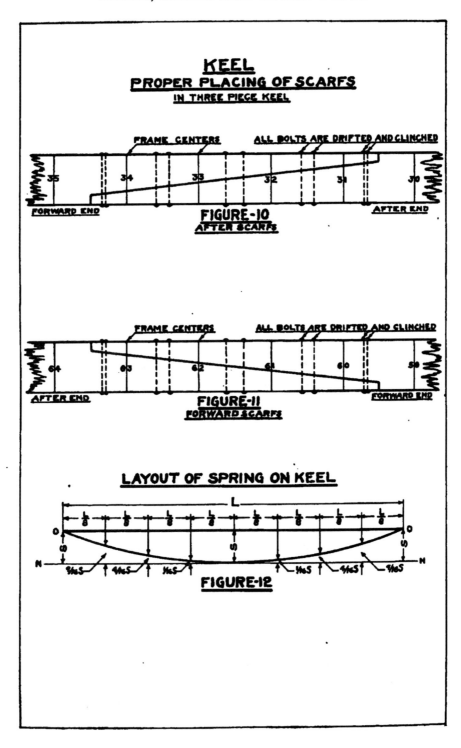

KEEL
PROPER PLACING OF SCARFS
IN THREE PIECE KEEL

FRAME CENTERS   ALL BOLTS ARE DRIFTED AND CLINCHED

35   34   33   32   31   30

FORWARD END   AFTER END

FIGURE-10
AFTER SCARFS

FRAME CENTERS   ALL BOLTS ARE DRIFTED AND CLINCHED

64   63   62   61   60   59

AFTER END   FORWARD END

FIGURE-11
FORWARD SCARFS

LAYOUT OF SPRING ON KEEL

FIGURE-12

longer, not shorter. The length of scarf to be used is generally indicated on the plans.

Keel scarfs must be clinch bolted. A common rule is two bolts between each frame. The plans should be carefully noted in this respect, as additional bolts are sometimes called for. These bolts, in so far as possible, should be kept clear of the frame landings and arranged as shown in Figs. 10 and 11.

The forward and middle scarfs are generally set as shown in Fig. 11. Sometimes the after scarf is reversed, as shown in Fig. 10. This permits the removal of the after piece of keel in case of damage without rescarfing the piece next to it. Where this is not done all scarfs will set as shown in Fig. 11.

Molds are furnished from the loft for the forward and after ends of the keel. These molds have the frame numbers scribed on them, and when matched up with the same frame numbers on the keel give the exact location of the cuts.

Three styles of forward ends are shown in Figs. 7, 8 and 9. These may be named in very much the same manner as scarfs. Fig. 7 would be called "plain," Fig. 8, "locked," and Fig. 9, "nibbed." The depth of nib or lock may be the same as that of nibs for scarfs, but in no case should it be less. Where the lock or nib is used, the rabbet lines are so adjusted in the loft that the outer rabbet line will cross well up on the lock, or nib, but not higher than the top of the keel. The use of the lock or nib properly arranged avoids the forming of a shim where the outer rabbet line leaves the keel. In the plain end, where this shim is always formed, some difficulty is often encountered by the shim starting to split out when the rabbet seam is calked.

The after end of the keel must be worked to receive the lower ends of the stern, or propeller post, and the rudder post, if one is to be fitted. These landings are very often called "steps."

If the vessel is a single-screw ship with a wood rudder, it will have a propeller post and a rudder post. The propeller

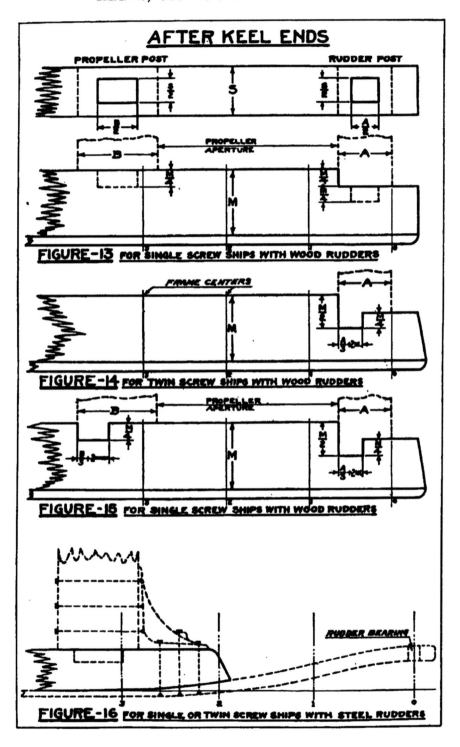

AFTER KEEL ENDS

FIGURE-13 FOR SINGLE SCREW SHIPS WITH WOOD RUDDERS

FIGURE-14 FOR TWIN SCREW SHIPS WITH WOOD RUDDERS

FIGURE-15 FOR SINGLE SCREW SHIPS WITH WOOD RUDDERS

FIGURE-16 FOR SINGLE OR TWIN SCREW SHIPS WITH STEEL RUDDERS

post is also the stern post. See Figs. 13 and 15. A single-screw ship with a steel rudder will have propeller post, which is also the stern post. See Fig. 16. A twin-screw ship, with a wood rudder, will have a stern post, which is also the rudder post, and will have no propeller post. See Fig. 14.

Fig. 13 shows the boxed, or blind, mortise step for stern and rudder posts. Figs. 14 and 15 show the open mortise step. Either of these steps may be used with any arrangement of posts. If a mold is not furnished for locating and marking out the steps, then the distance from a given frame center and the dimensions for the mortises are supplied from the loft, or drafting room. The proportions of mortise and step may or may not be indicated on the plans. Very often this is left to the judgment of the carpenter foreman. Good proportions are shown in Figs. 13, 14 and 15.

Fig. 16 shows an arrangement where a steel rudder is fitted. It will be noted that a steel shoe is used to carry the lower rudder bearing, and that the keel is extended abaft the post only far enough to receive a steel knee. In addition, there are steel side plates (not shown) extending from the shoe well up on each side of the stern post. All of the types shown are fitted with steel or bronze side plates extending along each side of the keel and well up on the stern and rudder posts. These will be more fully described later on.

The rabbet on the keel is laid out from offsets taken from the loft floor. The offsets give the distances in from the side for the inner rabbet line and down from the top for the outer rabbet line. Unless there is a back rabbet the surface between the two lines is cut straight. The offsets are taken at designated frame centers. Where there is a back rabbet, fids, or small molds, are prepared in the loft to fit the shape of the rabbet at about every other frame center. The inner and outer rabbet lines are then used as limit guides for the fids.

The rabbets at the extreme ends of the keel should not be cut until after the framing has been completed. Then, as the frames are dubbed, the rabbets are cut and faired.

As before mentioned, keels are laid without the shoe when the main keelson bolts are to be clinched under the keel. After the main keelsons are in place and fastened down, the keel is jacked up a section at a time and the shoe slipped into place in short pieces. Since the shoe is merely a fender for the keel it need not be in long lengths. It is fastened with common ship spikes, spaced about 12 inches apart and staggered.

After the keel has been laid on the blocks and the scarfs bolted up it must then be faired to the spring points. This is best done by means of an instrument called a transit, although it can be, and very often is, done by sighting with the eye. After fairing to the spring the keel must then be shored sideways until perfectly straight. If there is a taper in siding at each end, a full length centerline is scribed for this purpose. While a straight-sided keel can be sighted fairly well with the eye, a tapered keel should always be lined with a transit.

The proportions for spring points between the middle and the ends of the keel are shown in Fig. 12. The figure has, of course, been very much foreshortened to bring it within the limits of the page, but this does not alter the principle involved.

In the figure, S represents the amount of spring, and L the length of the keel. Example—Let S equal 5 inches and L equal 240 feet. Then L over 8 equals 30 feet; $\frac{1}{16}$ of S equals $\frac{5}{16}$ of one inch, $\frac{4}{16}$ of S equals $1\frac{1}{4}$ inches, and $\frac{9}{16}$ of S equals $2^{13}\!\!/_{16}$ inches. Therefore, the keel at a point 30 feet each way from the middle and lowest point will rise $\frac{5}{16}$ of one inch from the line N-N; 60 feet out from the middle it will rise $1\frac{1}{4}$ inches above the line N-N; 90 feet out, $2^{13}\!\!/_{16}$ inches, and 120 feet out 5 inches, or the full amount of the spring. Obviously, these offsets may be subtracted from 5 inches and the remainders measured down from the line O-O passing through the ends of the keel, and in practice this is the simpler way to do it.

STEMS

There are several good arrangements of stem construction in common use. A few of these are shown in Figs. 17, 18 and 19. In some cases the inner rabbet line is laid out on the joint between the stem and the apron, resulting in what is known as a free stem. See Fig. 18. It will be noted, in this case, that the planking merely butts against the stem and that all of the plank end fastening will land in the apron. The more common method is to lay out the rabbet well onto the stem, so as to get some of the plank end fastening into the stem proper.

Stems are not set up square off the keel, as this would make them appear to be leaning backward. Not only is the stem leaned, or raked forward, but very often the forward face is cut on a slight forward spring, or roman nosed, as it were, to avoid the hollow appearance which a perfectly straight stem has. In a stem 48 feet long the rake forward would be from 6 to 12 inches, and the spring about 1 to 1½ inches.

Molds, showing the exact shape of each piece of the stem structure, are furnished from the loft. These molds have the waterlines and frame centers marked upon them, and these lines should be transferred to the various pieces by the carpenter laying them out. They are used for future location of framing, etc. The molds also show the outer rabbet line and the bearding line. If the rabbet varies in depth this also will be marked, thus giving full information for laying out and cutting the rabbet. In addition, the width of the forward face of the stem and forefoot will be marked at frequent intervals on their respective molds. Since the tapered side of the stem always extends back to the outer rabbet line, this gives sufficient information for the shaping of that portion of the stem forward of the outer rabbet line. The siding of the stem in way of the outer rabbet line always remains constant, *i. e.*, it will be the same at top, middle and bottom.

The stem, apron and forefoot are assembled and bolted

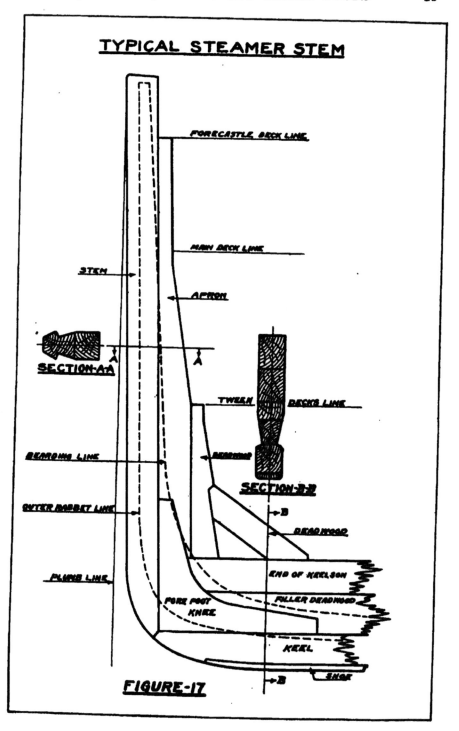

FIGURE-17

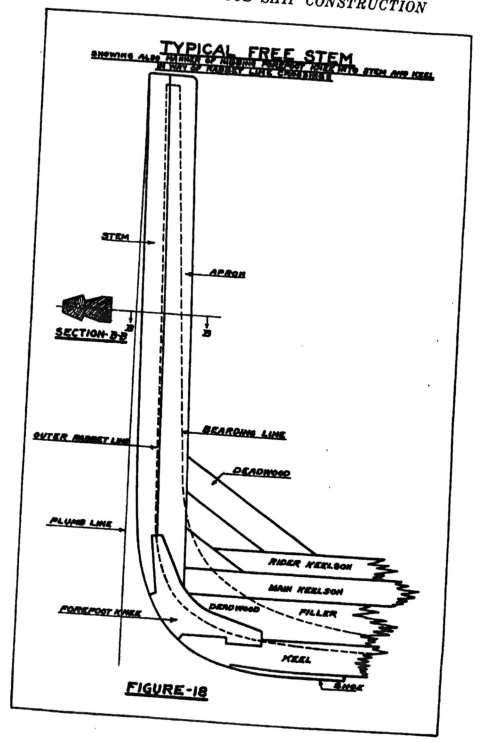

TYPICAL FREE STEM
SHOWING ALSO METHOD OF FITTING APRON OR KNEE INTO STEM AND KEEL
IN WAY OF RABBET LINE CONSTRUCT

STEM

APRON

SECTION-B-B

OUTER RABBET LINE

BEARDING LINE

DEADWOOD

PLUMB LINE

RIDER KEELSON

MAIN KEELSON

FOREFOOT KNEE

DEADWOOD

FILLER

KEEL

SHOE

FIGURE-18

together on the ground. If knightheads are fitted they are also worked out and fastened down to the apron at this time. (Knightheads are really a part of the frame and will be more fully described in the next chapter on framing.) Then, at the proper time, the entire stem structure is erected and shored in position. Three long, heavy shores are used—one forward and one on each side. Care must be taken to set the stem plumb and to the correct rake with the keel.

The straight rabbet on the stem is cut before erection. Below the turn of the forefoot it usually is not cut until the frame has been set up and is being dubbed. With careful loft work, however, the entire rabbet may be cut with very little danger of making a serious error.

The fastening of the stem at the forefoot must be carefully laid out, or it will be impossible to drive a sufficient number of bolts through. Stern and forefoot bolts, whenever possible, are driven through and clinched. An example of this fastening is shown in Fig. 20. Plans for this fastening are usually furnished and should be closely followed.

PROPELLER POSTS

Figs. 21 and 22 show two typical forms of stern, or propeller posts that are in common use. In Fig. 21 the post is cut off at and mortised into the horn timber, while in Fig. 22 it is extended upward between two horn timbers and connects to a deck beam. The two forms result in entirely different stern frame arrangements, which will be shown in the next chapter. The post in Fig. 21 is most commonly used in small, single-deck vessels, and that in Fig. 22 in larger vessels with more than one deck. Either post, however, may be used on large or small ships.

The figures show the posts as finished. Molds are furnished from the loft, giving the exact length and shape of the post, tenons at top and bottom, location and size of shaft hole, and the seat for the arch knee. As a rule the rabbets are not cut until the stern framing is completed, and then only as the dubbing proceeds, as it is difficult to

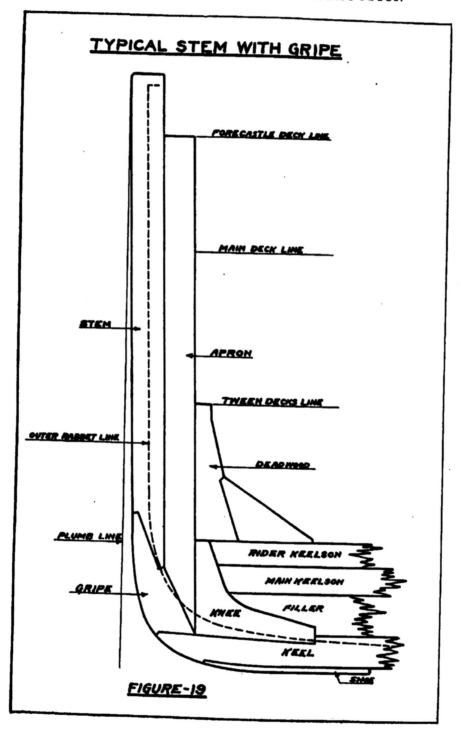

TYPICAL STEM WITH GRIPE

FORECASTLE DECK LINE

MAIN DECK LINE

STEM

APRON

TWEEN DECKS LINE

OUTER RABBET LINE

DEADWOOD

PLUMB LINE

RIDER KEELSON

MAIN KEELSON

GRIPE

FILLER

KNEE

KEEL

SHOE

FIGURE-19

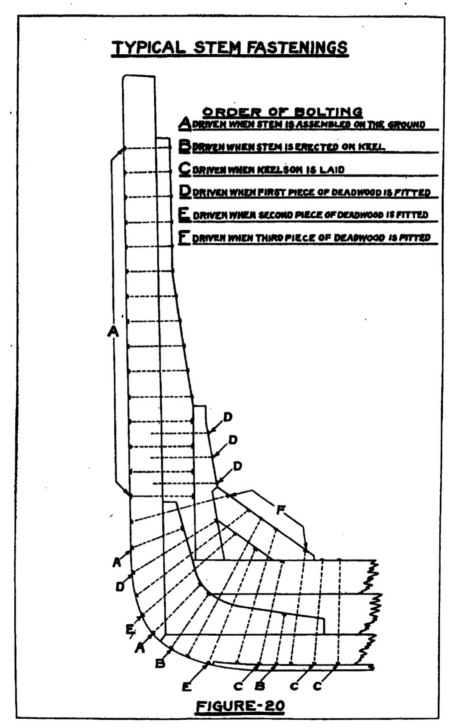

TYPICAL STEM FASTENINGS

ORDER OF BOLTING

A DRIVEN WHEN STEM IS ASSEMBLED ON THE GROUND

B DRIVEN WHEN STEM IS ERECTED ON KEEL

C DRIVEN WHEN KEELSON IS LAID

D DRIVEN WHEN FIRST PIECE OF DEADWOOD IS FITTED

E DRIVEN WHEN SECOND PIECE OF DEADWOOD IS FITTED

F DRIVEN WHEN THIRD PIECE OF DEADWOOD IS FITTED

FIGURE-20

2

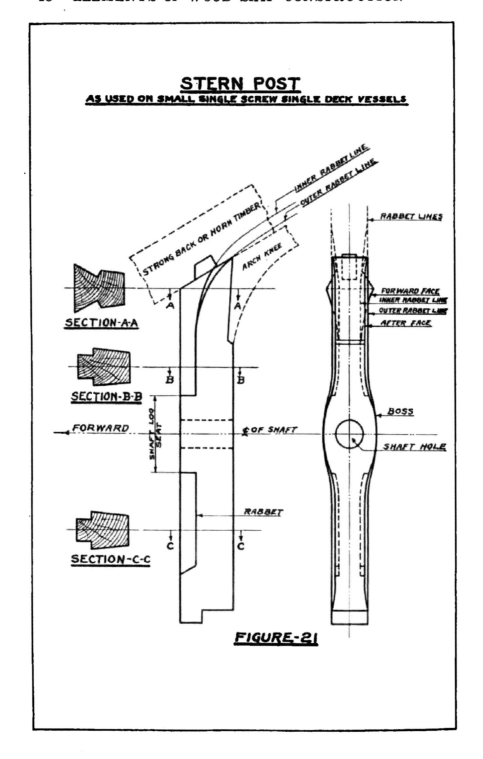

STERN POST

AS USED ON SMALL SINGLE SCREW SINGLE DECK VESSELS

FIGURE-21

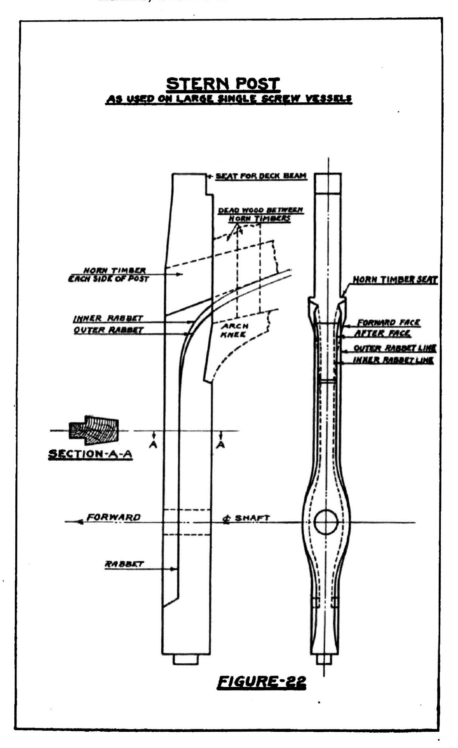

STERN POST
AS USED ON LARGE SINGLE SCREW VESSELS

FIGURE-22

lay them out with sufficient accuracy. But the shape of the post, in siding, can, and ought to be, roughed out a little over size, as this saves dubbing after erection. The post is not finally faired off to the shape shown in the figures until after the planking has been completed.

Where extreme care is taken in molding and setting the stern frame and in laying out the siding and rabbets on the post, the rabbets may be cut before the post is set up. Even in this case it is best to rough out the rabbets under-size, leaving the finishing operation until the dubbing is being done.

The post should be left full in siding forward of the rabbet at the top, so that most of the bearding will fall on the post. Where this is not done, *i. e.*, where the post is cut straight from top of boss to top, shims and chocks have to be fitted to take the plank end fastening. They make a poor job and, in addition, are very troublesome.

RUDDER POSTS

In single-screw vessels having a wood rudder there will be a rudder post abaft the stern post. The space between the two posts is called the propeller aperture. A typical construction for this post is shown in Fig. 23. The layout method for this post is the same as that described later for Fig. 25, although the construction of the trunk is different. Since the rabbet, in Fig. 23, crosses the trunk in a straight line and does not turn down onto the post, as shown in Fig. 25, the trunk can be built up, as shown in section A-A. This saves a great deal of labor and material, as the post can then be ordered to the siding of the lower end instead of to the siding of the trunk, and there will be no excess material on the lower end to be cut away. All of the joints in this trunk, as well as that shown in Fig. 25, should be well packed with white lead and cotton before bolting up. Very often, in addition to this, a seam is left, which is calked with oakum after bolting up.

The entire trunk must be clamped together hard before the holes are bored and the bolts driven and clinched.

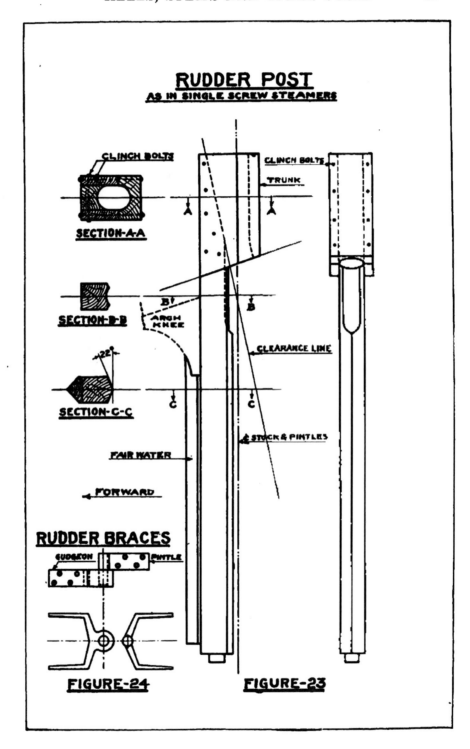

RUDDER POST

AS IN SINGLE SCREW STEAMERS

CLINCH BOLTS

SECTION-A-A

CLINCH BOLTS

TRUNK

SECTION-B-B

ARCH KNEE

CLEARANCE LINE

SECTION-C-C

STOCK & PINTLES

FAIR WATER

FORWARD

RUDDER BRACES

GUDGEON   PINTLE

FIGURE-24   FIGURE-23

Very often the main piece of this post is made of hard-wood. A fairwater is fitted on the forward side of all rudder posts, as shown in Fig. 23. This is spiked in place with ship spikes, after the arch knees have been fitted.

In twin-screw vessels with a wood rudder there will be a stern post, as shown in Fig. 25. An outline of the rudder blade and stock is also shown in this figure. Here, as shown in sections A-A and B-B, the main piece and forward part of the trunk are cut from a single timber. The afterpiece of the trunk is much the same as that shown in Fig. 23. Before the stern frame is complete, in this as in the propeller posts shown in Figs. 21 and 22, the rabbets are merely roughed out, or left uncut, the final cutting being done during the dubbing operation. The turn on the rabbet at the tuck should be roughed out quite full, as indicated in the figure.

To lay out the trunk and clearance line one must know the diameters of the stock and pintles and the location of the uppermost gudgeon. A detail drawing of the braces should also be available. A set of braces, consisting of gudgeon and pintle, are shown in Fig. 24.

The distance from the after side of the post to the center line of the stock and pintles is usually shown on the plans or can be taken from the detail drawing of the braces. However, in the absence of this information, it is usually made equal to one-half the diameter of the pintle plus $\frac{3}{8}$ of an inch to 1 inch for clearance.

The lap of the stock onto the blade should be, at least, from one-fourth to one-third the length of the blade measured in the same direction as the stock. This lap is often called the "plug." Sometimes the entire stock is so-called. The diameter of hole in the trunk, athwart-ships, should be equal to diameter of stock plus about 1 inch.

Then, to obtain the clearance, locate and draw outline of top gudgeon. From a point at the top of the post about 3 inches from the forward face draw a straight line N-N passing about $\frac{1}{2}$ inch outside the outline of the

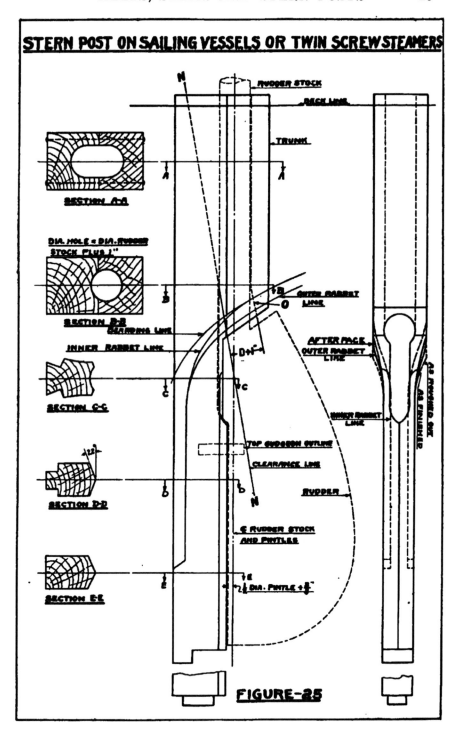

FIGURE-25

gudgeon. This line is the clearance line, and represents the foremost extent of the hole in the trunk required to clear the stock past the top gudgeon when shipping the rudder.

Then measure square out from the line N-N the distance, Dia. of stock plus 1 inch, and draw the short line O parallel to N-N. The line O then indicates the amount that must be removed from the lower after side of the trunk to clear the stock when shipping the rudder. The remainder of the hole in the trunk is obtained by measuring out each side from the centerline, the distance, ½ Dia. of stock plus ½ inch, and drawing parallel lines until they intersect the lines N-N and O. The forward one of these lines must be carried down on the main piece far enough to clear the plug. All of these lines are shown on the molds for the post and are readily transferred to the timbers.

The after face of the post below the trunk is bevelled off each side of the centerline to an angle of about 22 degrees, as shown in section D-D. Since the forward edge of the rudder is cut to the same bevels, and there is about ⅜ of an inch clearance between the rudder and the post, this permits the rudder to go over about 45 degrees each side of the centerline.

The travel of the rudder as given above is not necessarily the rule in all ships, and the plans should be carefully followed should other degrees of travel be specified.

SHAFT LOGS

Every powered vessel, whether single- or twin-screw, must be fitted with a shaft log or tube, for each shaft, so arranged as to provide support for the shaft bearings and secure watertightness where the shaft passes through the hull or deadwood. In a single-screw vessel the log will be on the centerline and will fit against or mortise into the stern post. Such a log is shown in Fig. 26. In a twin-screw vessel the log will pass through the hull some distance away from the centerline, but the construction of the log will be the same as that shown.

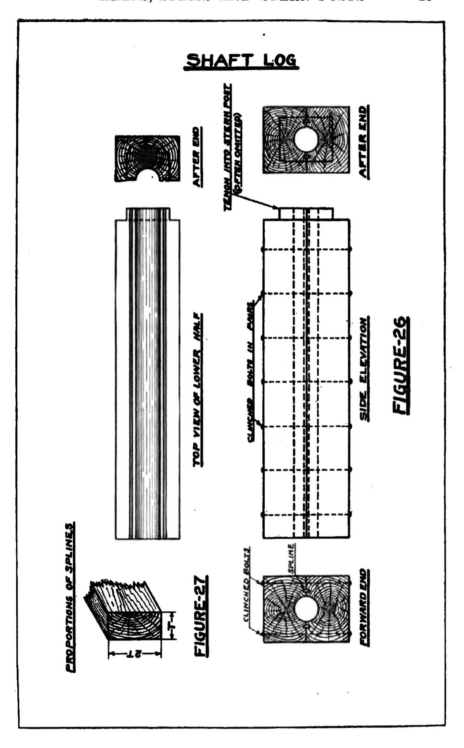

SHAFT LOG

TENON INTO STERN POST
(OFTEN OMITTED)

AFTER END

AFTER END

TOP VIEW OF LOWER HALF

CLINCHED BOLTS IN PAIRS

SIDE ELEVATION

FIGURE-26

PROPORTIONS OF SPLINES

FIGURE-27

CLINCHED BOLTS

SPLINE

FORWARD END

These logs, where not necessary to use four timbers, are built in halves, each half having exactly one-half of the hole cut in it. The joint between the two halves is arranged as a calking seam with an opening of about $\frac{3}{32}$-inch outside. In addition, it is customary to fit a soft wood spline on each side of the hole and inside of the line of bolts. If a good fit is secured these splines will make the log watertight without the calking. These logs are afterwards bored out perfectly true and fitted with lead or iron sleeves, which are watertight, but this does not relieve the workman from the necessity of making the log as tight as possible without the sleeve.

Logs may or may not be made with a tenon for mortising into the stern post. With careful workmanship the mortise makes the best job.

The bolting, or fastening, of the log varies with different ships. Logs made for insertion through the skin of the ship, as for twin-screws, are invariably bolted up as shown in the figure. Where possible, this should be done with centerline logs for single-screw ships. Where it is not possible to drive bolts from the top of the log, clear of the hole and into the deadwood below, then the lower half of the log is fastened in place first, bolts being driven through it and well into the deadwood below. Then the top half is fastened to the first half with bolts arranged as shown in the figure. These bolts cannot be clinched. In the majority of cases, however, the log can be bolted up before being placed in the ship. The two halves must be clamped together very tight before holes are bored, and bolts driven and clinched. Clinch rings should be set in flush.

GLOSSARY

Athwartship—Across the ship—at right angle to the keel.
Dimensions—Molded Length—The extreme distance from plank rabbet on the stem to the plank rabbet on the stern. Length between perpendiculars. The distance from the fore side of the stem to the after side of the rudder post, measured on the keel.
Molded Depth—The perpendicular distance amidship from the top

of the keel to the top of the main deck beam at the outside of the frame.

Depth of Hold—The perpendicular distance amidship, from the top of the bottom ceiling to the top of the main deck beam at the centerline.

Molded Beam—The width of the ship at the main deck taken amidship to the outside of the frame.

Breadth—Extreme—The greatest width of the ship over the planking.

Dub—To cut fair with an adz. Dubbing, in general, covers the operation of fairing up the frame of the ship inside and outside. Used in connection with any work performed with an adz.

Fay—To fit together. Faying surfaces are surfaces that must be fitted together, as in scarfs. To fay means to fit. Fayed means fitted. Both in the sense that fitting means the securing of good contact between the surfaces.

Fair—Smooth, without irregularities. A fair curve means a curve pleasing to the eye—without sudden sharp turns or humps.

Inboard—Inside the ship's. hull or superstructure. INBOARD SIDE means the side facing inboard, or toward the inside.

Midship—The center of the ship. AMIDSHIPS means at the center of the ship.

Molding—That dimension of a plank or timber reading from outboard to inboard.

Outboard—Outside the ship's hull or superstructure. OUTBOARD SIDE means the side facing outboard, or away from the inside.

Rabbet—In general, a recess, or groove, to receive the edges or ends of planking, siding, etc. A rabbet may be nothing more than a small surface squared off to receive a plank edge as in Fig. 28.

The rabbet in general is marked out by three lines, namely: The outer rabbet line, the inner rabbet line, and the bearding line. See Figs. 29 and 30. The surface between the inner and outer rabbet lines is called the rabbet. The surface between the inner rabbet line and the bearding line is called the bearding.

When the plank next to the keel, or the garboard, as it is called, is very thick, and the keel rather narrow in siding, a back rabbet is cut near the ends of the ship, to keep from cutting in too far in on the keel. The principal object of the rabbet as used on a ship's hull is to protect the plank ends and, permit calking. Therefore the rabbet must be nearly square with the surface of the plank fitting into it.

Scantlings—A term used in referring to the sizes of the various timbers comprising the ship's structure. The expression "Light scantling ship" means a ship with light timbers, etc.

Siding—The dimension of a timber reading opposite to the molding. Example: Keel sided 18 in., molded 24 in., means a keel having a depth of 24 in. and a width athwartship of 18 in.

Scribe—To mark one timber off against another, so that when the first timber is cut to the marks it will fit the second timber.

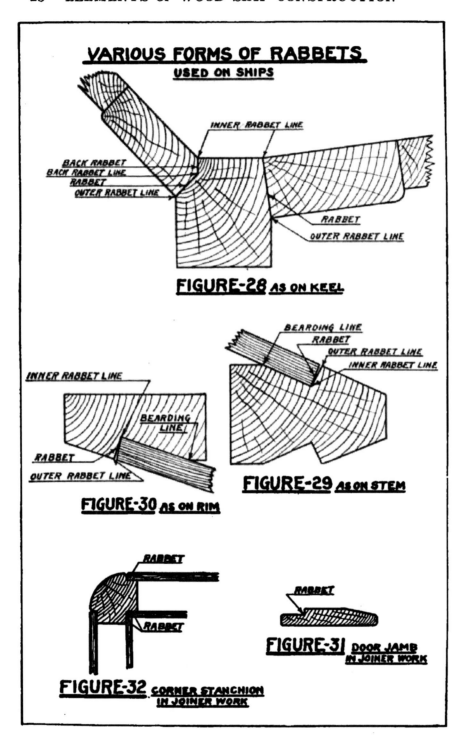

VARIOUS FORMS OF RABBETS
USED ON SHIPS

INNER RABBET LINE

BACK RABBET
BACK RABBET LINE
RABBET
OUTER RABBET LINE

RABBET
OUTER RABBET LINE

FIGURE-28 AS ON KEEL

BEARDING LINE
RABBET
OUTER RABBET LINE
INNER RABBET LINE

INNER RABBET LINE

BEARDING LINE

RABBET
OUTER RABBET LINE

FIGURE-30 AS ON RIM

FIGURE-29 AS ON STEM

RABBET

RABBET

RABBET

FIGURE-31 DOOR JAMB IN JOINER WORK

FIGURE-32 CORNER STANCHION IN JOINER WORK

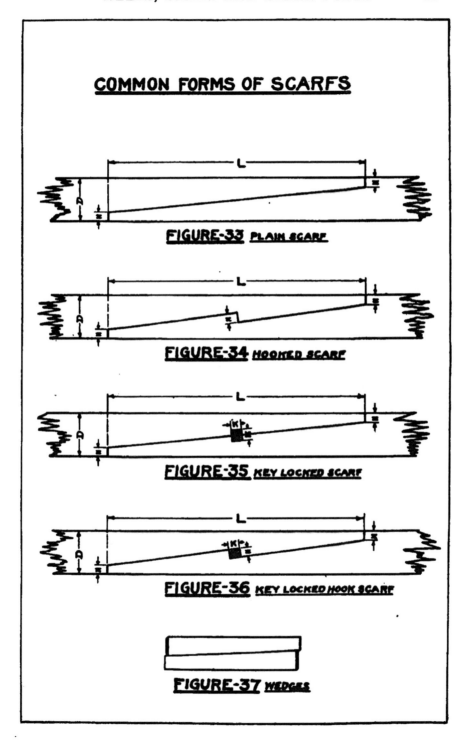

COMMON FORMS OF SCARFS

FIGURE-33 *PLAIN SCARF*

FIGURE-34 *HOOKED SCARF*

FIGURE-35 *KEY LOCKED SCARF*

FIGURE-36 *KEY LOCKED HOOK SCARF*

FIGURE-37 *WEDGES*

Ship—To place or mount on the ship. Shipping a rudder means placing the rudder in its position on the ship. Contrariwise to unship anything, means to take it from its position on the ship.

Scarf—To join together with an overlap. Joints between timbers, as shown in Figs. 33 to 36 inclusive. These figures show the four principal forms of scarfs used in shipbuilding. Several modifications of these forms are also used, which will be shown later on.

Timbers are scarfed to secure strength and it is therefor important that the proportions of the scarf be correct. The length should not be less than six times the depth, the depth being measured as indicated by the letter D in the figures.

The nib should be about 25 per cent. of the depth "D." The following formula will be found to give excellent proportions for all ordinary scarfs.

Let $\rrbracket$ D = Depth of Scarf.
  L = Length of Scarf.
  N = Depth of Nib.
  K = Width of Key.

Then L = 6 × D

$$N = \frac{D}{8} + 1 \text{ in., where D is 8 in. or more.}$$

$$N = \frac{D}{4} \text{ where D is less than 8 in.}$$

$$K = \frac{D}{4}$$

Keys for keyed scarfs are made of hardwood. They should be made in two pieces, wedge shaped, with a taper of about ½ inch to the foot, as shown in Fig. 37, and should be driven simultaneously from each side of the timber until very tight, then sawed off flush and wedged at the small ends so that they cannot possibly back out.

Flat and Edge Scarf—A scarf is called flat when the depth, or dimension D, reads across the edge, or narrow face of the timber.

An edge scarf is one where the dimension D reads across the side, or wide face of the timber.

FOREWORD TO CHAPTER II

As nearly as possible, in these chapters, the various features of the ship will be discussed in their order of erection, or emplacement, upon the vessel. This is not altogether possible, as many items may be in the course of preparation at the same time.

In the first chapter keels, stems, stern- and rudder-posts, and shaft-logs were discussed in general, and while the keel is the first item erected, the other pieces mentioned are, or should be, in the course of preparation at the same time. Simultaneously with this work the frames are being molded and sawn. As soon as the keel is laid and properly lined, the framing stage is set up, and the square frames assembled and erected. Then the framing stage is torn down and the stem and main stern-frame are erected and shored in position. Fitting the half-frames and cants then completes the vessel's frame, but before this can be done the keelsons must have been laid and all the dead-woods placed and fastened. Keelsons will be discussed in the next chapter.

In this chapter various features of the vessel's frame are discussed. While several types of frames are shown, it should be borne in mind that there are many variations which may be used without changing the principles involved.

Tabulation of the Order of Procedure to Complete the Frame

Main Operation	Coincident Operation
Setting of keel blocks.	Preparation of keel.
Laying of keel.	Molding and sawing of frames.
Erection of framing stage.	Preparation of stem structure, stern-post, rudder-post, and stern-frame parts.
Assembling and erecting square-frames.	
Erection of stem structure, stern-post and stern-frame parts.	Preparation of main and sister keelsons.
Laying of main keelsons.	Assembly of half frames or cants.
Erection of cants and half frames.	

CHAPTER II

FRAMES IN GENERAL

All ship frames are usually built double, that is, of two tiers of timbers, so arranged that the timbers of one tier overlap the butts of the timbers in the other tier. The various timbers of the frame are sawn to proper shape and bevel from stock called "flitch." Flitch may be ordered rough sawn, or planed on one or both sides. Planed flitch is coming more into use, as it is easier to mold and work.

It will be remembered then that a frame consists of two tiers of timbers, and that when we speak of a timber in general reference to the frame, we mean one-half of the frame at the point under discussion. For instance, if plank fastening were specified two fastenings per timber, it would mean four to each frame.

For purposes of identification in working and assembling, the various timbers of the frame have been named. Referring to Fig. 38 it will be seen that the timbers crossing the keel are called floors. The uppermost timbers are called top timbers and the timbers between the floors and the top timbers are called futtocks. When a vessel has a bulwark where only one timber extends above the deck, this timber becomes a stanchion. Then there will be floors, futtocks, top timbers and stanchions, all in the same frame.

Inasmuch as half frames and cants do not cross the keel they have no floors and will consist of futtocks and top timbers only.

The futtocks are numbered, beginning with No. 1 for the futtock abutting the floor nearest the center line of the ship. In half frames and cants the shorter of the two futtocks abutting the deadwood is called No. 1. (See

32

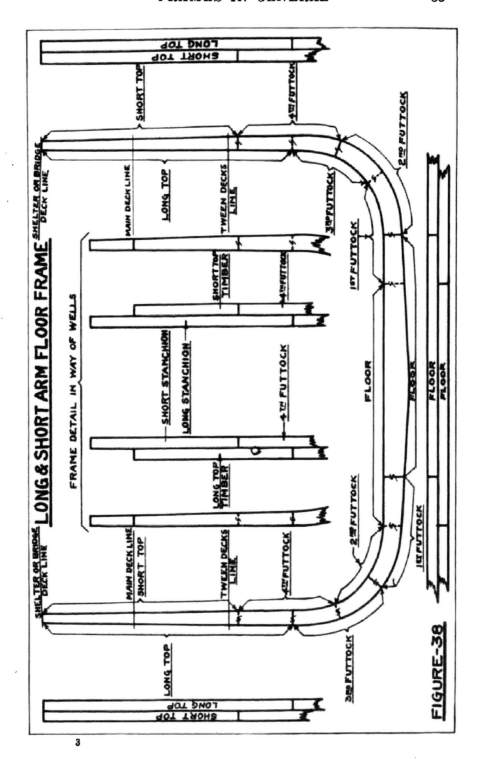

LONG & SHORT ARM FLOOR FRAME

FRAME DETAIL IN WAY OF WELLS

FIGURE-38

Figs. 44 and 45.) They are numbered thence in order up to the top timbers. It will be seen that on the same side of the ship the first, third and fifth futtocks will be in one tier, and the second, fourth and sixth futtocks in the other tier. First futtocks or futtocks of the same number may not be in the same tier on both sides of the ship, as will be seen later on.

SQUARE FRAMES

Square frames may be divided roughly into two types; namely, those having long and short arm floors, and those having long and short floors. Figure 38 shows a typical long and short arm floor midship frame. In this arrangement both floors are the same length, each being molded with a short arm on one side of the center line and a long arm on the other, and so placed that the short arm of one floor extends on the same side of the center line as the long arm of the other floor. The long arm of each floor thus furnishes a lap for attaching the first futtock. While it is common in large vessels to keep the deadrise down so that the floors amidship may be made straight on top without tapering too much toward the bilge, this type of floor may be used for boats having considerable deadrise. The top will then no longer be straight but would have the general appearance shown in Fig. 41.

In this type of frame it will be noticed that the first futtock on one side is in the same tier as the second futtock on the other side. (It is customary to refer to these tiers as upper and lower, and for clearness hereafter, timbers having butts shown dotted on the plates will be considered as being in the lower tier, while timbers having butts shown in solid lines will be in the upper tier.) Then, keeping in mind the location of the tiers, on one side of this frame in the lower tier there will be the first and third futtocks and a long top timber, while on the other side in the same tier there will be the second and fourth futtocks and a short top timber. When the frame happens to be in way of a well where there is a bulwark, then the long top timber will

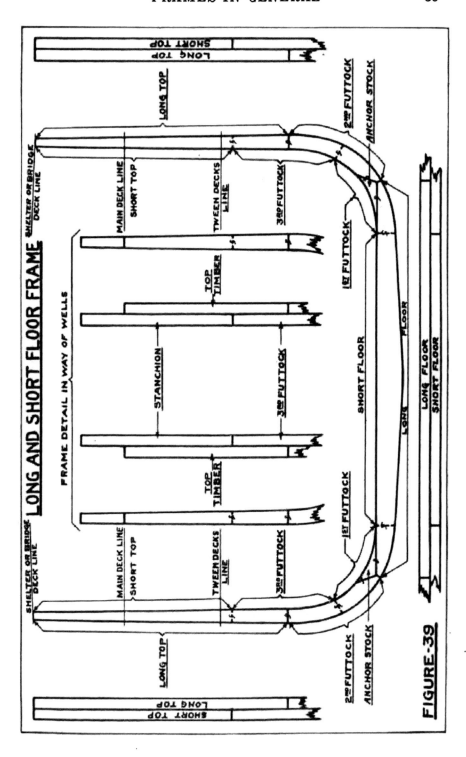

FIGURE-39

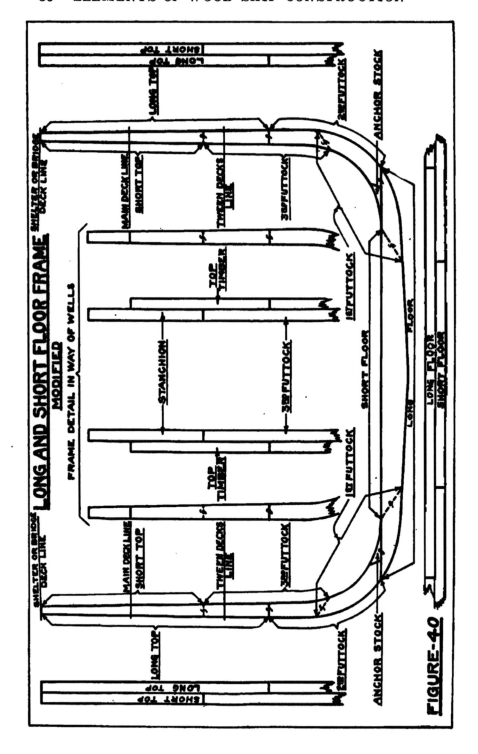

FIGURE-40

become a long stanchion, and the short timber a short stanchion. Stanchions generally are placed in the same tier on all frames. In short, futtocks and tops of the same number and name occurring in the lower tier on one side of this frame will occur in the upper tier on the other side.

Figure 39 shows a midship frame having long and short floors. This type of frame can be used only where the vessel has small deadrise so that the tops of the floors may be left straight. In the figure the short floor is shown in the lower tier and the long floor in the upper tier, the extension of the long floor past the ends of the short floor furnishing the lap for attaching the first futtocks. In this style of frame, futtocks of like numbers and tops of same name will fall in the same tier. Also, stanchions will be of the same length should the frame call for them. Hence this frame is much simpler to assemble than the long and short arm floor frame.

It will be noticed that the second futtocks in this frame abut the ends of the long floor and that an anchor stock is used to fill out this tier flush with the inside of the first futtock in the lower tier. This construction forms a short scarf at the bilge, which, after the ceiling and planking bolts have been driven through it, tends to increase the strength of the frame at this point.

Figure 40 shows a modification of the long and short floor frame, which, however, is seldom used because of the trouble experienced in fitting the butts in the vicinity of the bilge. Here the first futtock is scarfed to the short floor and third futtock, while the second futtock lands on top of the long floor. The anchor stock is much smaller than that shown in Fig. 39 and might be more properly called a chock. The only difference between the two frames shown in Figs. 39 and 40 is in the arrangement of the butts around the bilge.

No matter what type of frame is used amidship, as soon as points forward and aft are reached where the deadrise increases rapidly, or the frame assumes the general shape shown in Fig. 41, it is necessary to use long and short arm

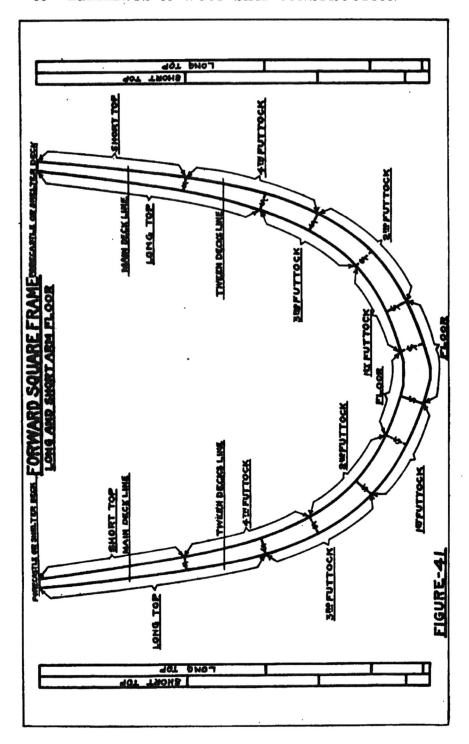

FIGURE-41

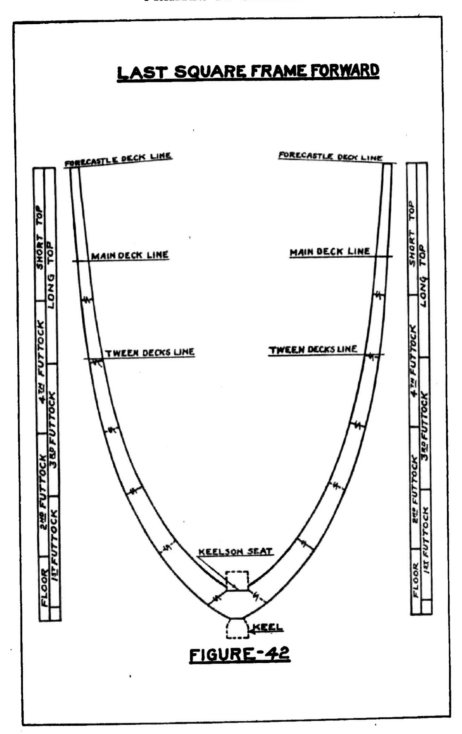

LAST SQUARE FRAME FORWARD

FORECASTLE DECK LINE

MAIN DECK LINE

TWEEN DECKS LINE

KEELSON SEAT

KEEL

SHORT TOP · LONG TOP · 4TH FUTTOCK · 3RD FUTTOCK · 2ND FUTTOCK · 1ST FUTTOCK · FLOOR

FIGURE-42

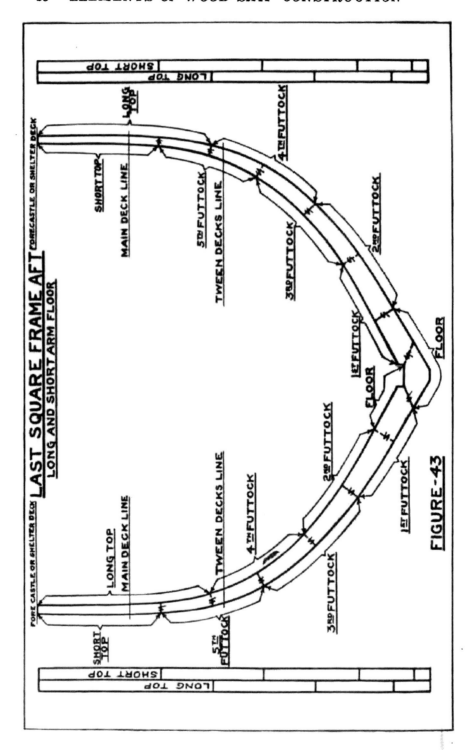

FIGURE-43

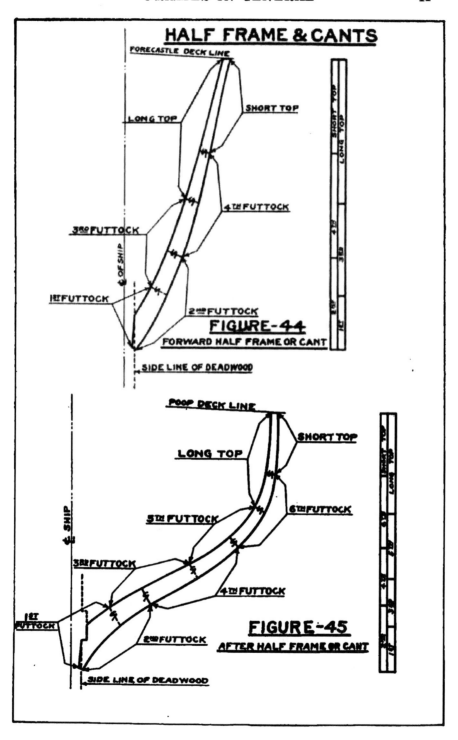

HALF FRAME & CANTS

FORECASTLE DECK LINE

SHORT TOP

LONG TOP

4TH FUTTOCK

3RD FUTTOCK

₵ OF SHIP

1ST FUTTOCK

2ND FUTTOCK

FIGURE-44

FORWARD HALF FRAME OR CANT

SIDE LINE OF DEADWOOD

POOP DECK LINE

SHORT TOP

LONG TOP

₵ SHIP

5TH FUTTOCK

6TH FUTTOCK

3RD FUTTOCK

4TH FUTTOCK

1ST FUTTOCK

2ND FUTTOCK

FIGURE-45

AFTER HALF FRAME OR CANT

SIDE LINE OF DEADWOOD

floors to secure frames of the greatest strength. As the last square frames forward and aft are approached they will assume the general forms shown in Figs. 42 and 43. It will then be found best and most economical to mold the long and short arm floors as indicated in these figures.

So far, in all of the frames discussed, the timbers have been sawn from straight-grained flitch. In some localities, such as the coast of Maine, the bilge futtocks, where the frame is not too large, are molded from oak natural crooks. On the Pacific Coast, where very large natural crook fir knees are available, the long and short arm floors for such frames as those shown in Figs. 42 and 43 are sometimes made from knees. In this case the short arms would have butts square with the frame.

MOLDING

The operation of marking out the timbers of the frame by means of patterns or molds furnished from the loft is called "molding." It is a highly specialized operation, requiring some knowledge of lofting and a systematic and methodical procedure. The molder must not only keep an accurate record of each timber molded, and of the number of timbers to the frame, but must be able to utilize the ordered flitch to the best advantage and with the least possible waste.

There are two general schemes of building molds for frames. The first is to have three molds for each frame, a floor mold, one mold from the floor to and around the bilge, and the third mold thence to top of the frame. On these molds the various timbers are marked and numbered or named.

The second scheme is to have a mold for each timber of the frame. These are more convenient to handle and do not require as great skill in handling as molds built under the first scheme.

Slight variations of each of these two systems are also often used.

Complete information for the proper laying out and

marking of each timber appears on the molds. Molds need not necessarily be made to full width of the timber and, in fact, are not commonly so made. The outside edge of the mold is made true to the shape of the outside of the frame, while the inside edge may be scribed off inside of the inner line of the frame as much as six or eight inches. This is done solely to reduce the width of the mold and save mold lumber. In marking out a timber from a mold so made, the outer edge and butts are scribed direct from the mold, while the inner edge is scribed by means of a distance piece from the inside of the mold, thus accomplishing the same result as if the mold were full size.

The following information is marked on each mold: First, the exact location of each butt; second, the number or name of the futtock or timber on each side of the butt; third, the bevel at frequent intervals to which the timber is to be sawn; fourth, the number of the frame to which the timber belongs; fifth, if the mold is a floor mold it will have scribed upon it the center line corresponding to the center line of the keel; sixth, if the mold falls in way of a horning point not on a butt, the point will be scribed and marked with its number; seventh, molds for the lower futtocks of half-frames and cants usually have one or two waterlines scribed on them which should be transferred to the timbers to assist in placing the frame; eighth, the various deck lines are usually scribed on the mold, landing in their way, although only the uppermost one is customarily scribed onto the top timbers or stanchions when they are molded.

Timbers are always molded on the faces that fit together when assembled in the frame, hence the bevel marked on the timbers from the mold will read from the center of the frame forward in one tier of timbers and from the center of the frame aft in the other tier, and if the lower tier carries an under bevel, the upper tier will have a standing bevel, or vice versa.

Bevels on molds for long and short arm floor frames should not be marked standing or under. Bevels on molds for single futtocks in frames having long and short floors may be marked standing or under, but if the mold covers more than a single futtock it is not so marked. The reasons for these rules will be seen in the following examples:—

Suppose that the first futtocks in Fig. 38 are being molded and that the futtock in the lower tier has an under bevel. Then after molding this futtock and marking it with under bevels the first futtock in the top tier on the other side of the frame is marked out with the mold same side up, but with the bevels marked standing. And likewise with the third futtock and long top. Hence it will be seen that from the same face of the mold or molds we may mold all of the timbers of same number and name and it is not necessary to mark all of the butts on both sides of the mold. Putting it another way, from the same face of the molds we can mold the top tier on one side of the frame and the bottom tier on the other side. Since these tiers have like numbered futtocks they need be marked only on the one side of the mold, the opposite tiers being marked on the other side. With a mold so marked it is only necessary to mold a given timber, once with the bevels marked under, and once with the bevels marked standing, provided, of course, that the bevel is not square, and no care need be taken to definitely locate the timber in a given tier. The same rule applies to the floors. The above applies to molds covering more than a single timber. If individual molds are used for each timber they would be marked only on one side, and the rules for bevels would remain the same.

For another example take the molding of the first futtocks in Fig. 39. Here the futtocks are in the same tier and both will be assumed to have an under bevel. Then from one side of the mold the futtock to the right would be molded and marked with under bevels, then the mold must be turned over and the futtock to the left molded with the same under bevels. Since the mold must be turned over for each futtock molded it is necessary to mark all futtocks in both tiers on each side of the molds. And if the mold covers more than one timber, then from the same side of the mold would be molded the first futtock on one side of the frame with an under bevel, and the second futtock on the other side of the frame and in the top tier, with a standing bevel, hence the bevels may not be marked standing or under on the mold, unless it is an individual mold for a given futtock only. It is also necessary in this style of frame for the molder to fix the tier in which the first futtock, or any timber for that matter, is located, so that he may know whether to mark it standing or under bevel.

From the above the following rules may be evolved for molding frame timbers:

(1) In frames where like timbers fall in opposite tiers, mold like timbers from same side of mold, but with opposite bevels.

(2) In frames where like timbers fall in same tier, mold like timbers from opposite side of mold, but with same bevels.

BEVELS AND MARKS

Bevels are marked in degrees followed by letter "U" for under and "S" for standing; "2½ U" means two and one-half degrees under, and "3 S" means three degrees standing. Where there is no bevel, that is, where the timber is to be sawn square, it is marked with a cross in a circle thus ⊗

The principles involved in lifting frame bevels from the floor are very simple and should be understood by all ship carpenters, as they are frequently of use in operations other than framing.

Figure 46 shows a section and part of the plan of two frames. On the loft floor body plan only the lines M-M and N-N appear and the problem is to determine the proper bevel in degrees for the frame by measuring the distance between these lines. In this figure, A represents the distance between centers of frames, B the distance at one

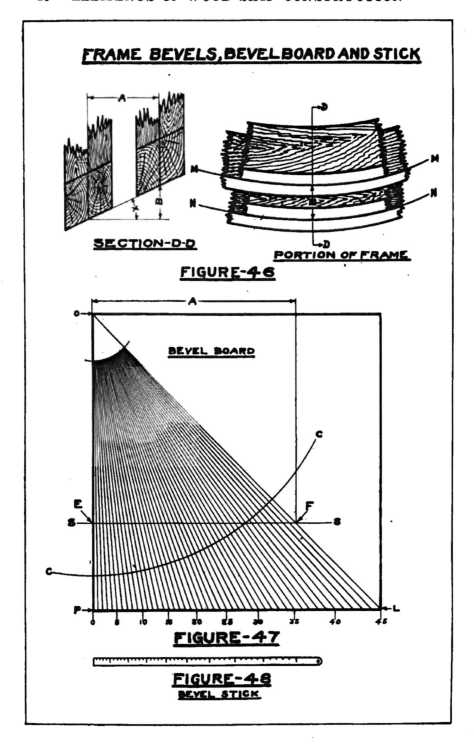

FRAME BEVELS, BEVEL BOARD AND STICK

SECTION-D-D

PORTION OF FRAME

FIGURE-46

BEVEL BOARD

FIGURE-47

FIGURE-48

BEVEL STICK

point between the lines M-M and N-N, and X the angle which it is desired to find, by measuring the distance B.

The first step is to construct a bevel board as shown in Fig. 47 as follows: Build up a square board having sides somewhat greater than the distance between frame centers. The board should have a smooth top, and be perfectly square, or have a perfect square scribed upon it, in which latter case the scribed square is considered as the extent of the board.

Then from the corner O draw a straight line to the corner L. This line will make an angle of 45 degrees with the side O-P. Next, with O as the center, draw any arc C-C, preferably with as large a radius as can be used on the board. Divide this arc between the lines O-L and O-P into 45 equal parts. Then each part represents a degree. Through each degree mark on the arc C-C draw a straight line from the center O extended to the side P-L.

The lines should then be numbered from 0 to 45, beginning with the side O-P as 0.

The next step is to lay out the bevel stick. Each different distance between frame centers will call for a different bevel stick, but they may all be taken off the same bevel board. In this case the distance between the frame centers is represented by the letter A, which represents the actual distance between the frames of the ship where bevels are desired.

Measure in from O on the top of the board, the distance A, and draw a line parallel to the side O-P, or square with the top, until it meets the line O-L at the point F. Through F draw line S-S parallel to the top of the board and square with the side O-P. This line between the points F and E will be the same length as the distance between the frame centers, and the points where the degree lines cross it are transferred to the bevel stick shown in Fig. 48, and numbered from 0 to 45.

Now, if the distance B be measured with this stick the degrees of the angle X may be read directly from the stick. If the lines M-M and N-N are very close together the bevel will be small, if far apart the bevel will be large, and if they are coincident, that is one over the other so that they appear as the same line, there will be no bevel and the timbers will be sawn square.

FRAME HORNING AND ASSEMBLING

As soon as the keel has been laid a framing stage is erected over the forward end of the keel, as shown in Figs. 49 and 50. In some yards a stage is built at each end of the keel and two framing crews are operated.

While the framing stage is a temporary structure, it should be strongly built and braced. The decking should not be less than three inches thick. The deck is usually laid over the top of the keel, as this makes it easier to slide the frame off the stage after it has been assembled.

The stage should be large enough to afford ample working room around the largest frames in the vessel. Sufficient blocks, about six to eight inches square and three to four feet in length, are provided to support and even up the first tier of timbers, as shown in Fig. 49. A center board from 12 to 16 inches wide and of the required length is fitted to receive the two horning points O and L. The distance between these points is furnished from the loft. The top of the center-board should be even with the top of the lower tier of the timbers after they have been laid up on the blocks.

In the frame shown in Fig. 49 there are four horning points, and one half-breadth point at the upper deck line. The figure shows the lower tier of a long and short arm floor frame and where the horning points do not land at the butts they are shown scribed on the timbers and numbered. It will be noted that three points on one side and one point on the other side of the frame land away from the butts. This would not necessarily occur in all long and short arm floor frames, but in any event where the horning points do not land at butts they are scribed on the timber and marked with the proper number.

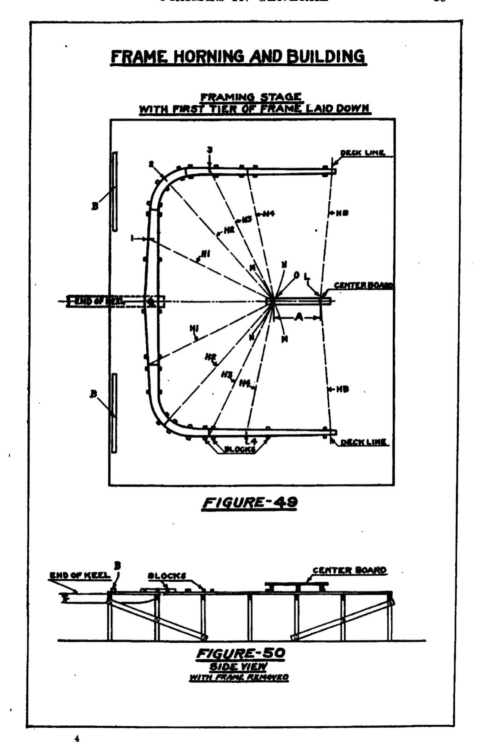

FRAME HORNING AND BUILDING

FRAMING STAGE
WITH FIRST TIER OF FRAME LAID DOWN

FIGURE-49

FIGURE-50
SIDE VIEW
WITH FRAME REMOVED

H1, H2, H3, and H4 represent horning diagonals, and these may or may not remain in the same relative position. In square frames forward and aft it is sometimes advisable to carry the horning points further up on the frame, but if the horning points are properly marked on the timbers this will not change the system of horning, or cause confusion.

A long square pole called a horning batten is furnished from the loft, and has each of the four sides numbered respectively 1, 2, 3, 4, to indicate the horning diagonal it represents. From the same end of this batten are marked the proper horning distances; that is, on the side numbered 1, the various lengths of H1 from the center O to the outer and upper corner of the lower tier at the first horning point are scribed and each distance marked with the number of the frame for which it is to be used. On the side numbered 2, the various lengths of H2 are scribed and marked in the same manner, and so on with H3 and H4, all being measured from the same end of the batten. A separate batten, called the half-breadth batten, is furnished for the half breadths at the deck and it is scribed and marked in the same manner as the horning batten. Now, with the stage prepared and equipped with center-board, blocks, etc., and with horning and half-breadth battens at hand, the assembling of the frame will proceed.

Assume that the number of the frame to be assembled is 10. The lower tier will be assembled as follows: First the floor is placed upon the blocks approximately in its proper position. Then with the horning batten, using the distance H1 marked for this frame, scribe arcs M-M and N-N across the center board from the horning points No. 1 as centers. Note that one of these centers falls at a butt and has, therefore, not been numbered in the figure. Where the two arcs cross drive a nail. Next, with a fine line, or straight edge, laid against the nail, and on the center-line scribed across the floor, draw the center-line shown on the center-board, measure up from the nail the distance A, which is furnished from the loft, and drive another nail. In practice the line is not drawn on the center-board, and the distance

A is measured along the line or straight edge held in proper position. As soon as it has been found that the arcs will cross on the center-board the floor is dogged fast so that it cannot move, and the arcs and measurements for the two points on the center-board should not be finally taken until the floor has been dogged.

Next, on the one side the first futtock is laid down on the blocks and brought into position so that its lower butt fits the butt of the floor, while the upper butt is shifted until, with the end of the horning batten held against the nail at O, its outer and upper corner corresponds with the measurement H2 indicated for this frame. The futtock is then lightly dogged in position. Next the second futtock on the opposite side is laid on the blocks and brought into position with its lower butt fitting the butt of the floor, while the upper end is shifted until, with the end of the horning batten held against the nail at O the outer and upper edge at horning point No. 2 corresponds with the distance H2 marked for that frame. Then this futtock is lightly dogged in place. Exactly the same procedure is followed in locating the balance of the futtocks in this tier and the lower ends of the top timbers. · When the top timbers are placed, the top is shifted until, with the half-breadth batten held against the nail at L, the outer and upper edge at the deck line corresponds with the half-breadth distance marked for this frame.

In placing the first tier of futtocks, if rough sawn timbers are used, thin shims must be used to bring the upper surfaces even. Shingles are best for this purpose.

After the first horning is completed, the butts are cut in with a large cross-cut saw until they fit when the timbers are driven together. With an experienced crew the cutting in of the butts will begin as soon as the first futtock has been dogged down. After the butts have been cut in until they fit and all of the timbers driven down, then the horning points and half-breadths are checked, and the timbers dogged fast.

This completes the assembling of the lower tier. The

upper tier timbers are laid on the lower tier in their proper position, so that the sawn edges match. They are then lightly dogged down until the butts have been cut in and the timbers are driven down, after which the dogs are driven tight. The frame is then bored and fastened. To hold the upper ends of the frame in position a lighter timber, called a cross-pawl, extending from top to top, must be spiked in place before the frame is moved from the stage. This cross-pawl usually consists of a 2″ × 8″ plank, either in one or two lengths, and should be well spiked to each top with ship spikes driven through washers. If the cross-pawl is made of two lengths of plank they should be well lapped and spiked at the joint.

 Frames are commonly skidded from the stage to their proper positions in the ship then up-ended into place. For this purpose a skid rail is erected on each side of the keel, its top being level with the top of the keel, and its distance out from the keel two or three feet less than the half breadth of the widest frame. Then a shoe is built to slide on the keel. This should have shrouds to keep it from sliding off to one side. As the frame is dragged from the stage with the yard winch tackle, this shoe is inserted under the floor. Just before the tops of the frame leave the stage a heavy timber, long enough to span the frame and skid rails, is inserted under and across the frame, a short distance from the top. The blocks marked B in Fig. 49 are for the purpose of holding the top of the frame clear of the stage and skid rails to permit the insertion of this timber. Supported in this fashion the frame is skidded to its proper position and up-ended.

FRAME TIMBER FASTENING

Frame fastening is clustered about the butt, as shown in Fig. 60. The figure shows six fastenings to the butt, but this number may be more or less, according to the size of the frame and the location of the butt in the frame. In large frames six or more may be driven at the floor butts, six in butts at the bilge, and four to the butt above the bilge. It is necessary, of course, to drive enough fastening in the frame to hold it in shape while it is being erected.

Four styles of fastening are used, namely; hardwood treenails, fir or pine treenails, iron drift bolts; and screw bolts. The screw bolts are generally machine bolts with square heads and nuts, with washers on each end. The screw-bolt fastening is the best for holding the frame in shape, while fir and pine treenails are the poorest for this purpose. Very often a combination of hardwood and softwood treenails are used, the hardwood treenails being used where the strains are the greatest.

PLUMBING AND SQUARING THE FIRST SQUARE FRAME

The first square frame set up must be squared with the keel. Since the keel has a declivity, and in addition is laid with a spring, this cannot be done by the ordinary method of squaring. While there are several methods of going about this problem, the following, as shown in Figs. 51, 52 and 53, is the best that has come to the author's attention. Figure 51 is a view looking down on top of the frame, square with the keel. Figure 52 is an elevation looking along the keel, and Fig. 53 is an elevation looking across the keel. For the purpose of illustration a definite example has been taken, the problem being to erect and square the first square frame on a keel having a slope of $\frac{5}{8}''$ to the foot, the keel having a spring and a taper. It is, therefore, impossible to square off either the sides or the top of this keel. We then proceed as follows:

With the frame set up in approximate position and at its proper location on the keel, set a straight edge having a length greater then the span of the frame across the keel and 24 inches away from the center of the frame. Square this straight edge with the center-line on the keel and level it by any of the methods well known to carpenters. Place a nail at center of frame, on each side, 16 feet above the top of the keel, care being taken to have the nail on each side

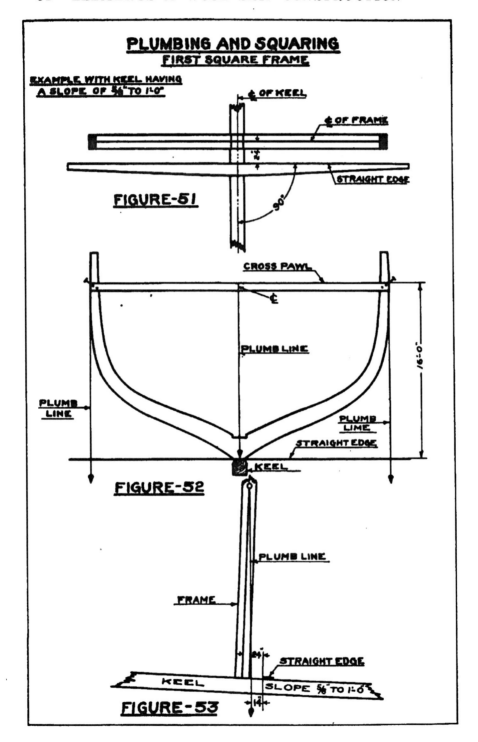

PLUMBING AND SQUARING
FIRST SQUARE FRAME

EXAMPLE WITH KEEL HAVING
A SLOPE OF 5/8" TO 1'-0"

FIGURE-51

FIGURE-52

FIGURE-53

exactly the same distance down from the deck line and 16 feet above the top of the keel. From each of these nails hang a plumb-bob with a line long enough to pass the ends of the straight edge. From the center of the cross-pawl hang another plumb-bob with plumb just short of the inside of the frame over the keel. Now, the nails at the sides of the frame are 16 feet above the straight edge and the slope of the keel is $\frac{5}{8}''$ to the foot. The slope in 16 feet will be 10 inches, and the side plumb-lines should be 10 inches nearer, or further away from the straight edge than the distance from the straight edge to the center of the frame at the keel, according to the position of the straight edge above or below the frame. In this case the straight edge has been placed below the frame, and the distance from the plumb-line to the straight edge will be 10 inches less than that at the keel, between the center of the frame and the straight edge, or 14 inches. Then all that is necessary to properly square the frame is to adjust the shores holding the frame in position until each of the side plumb-lines is 14 inches away from the straight edge, and the center plumb-bob hangs directly on the center-line of the keel.

This frame must be very rigidly shored in position. Then the balance of the frames are spaced from it with a space-stick reaching from center to center. If the spacing is carefully done it may not be necessary to make further checks for plumbing and squaring, but it is usually advisable to plumb and square by the above method at least three frames having some distance between them; that is, the last square-frame at each end and one at the midship.

All frames, as soon as erected on the keel, are plumbed and spaced from the last frame and fitted with bilge shores and cleats to hold them plumb and at proper space. Sometimes two sets of bilge shores are fitted. As soon as a number of the square-frames are up the ribbanding should be begun. Ribbands should be heavy enough and close enough together to properly bring the frames into alignment. Of course no amount of ribbanding can bring a

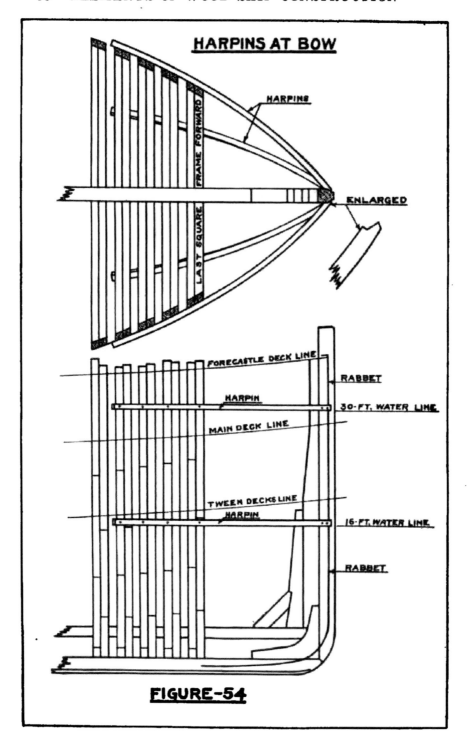

FIGURE-54

poorly molded and assembled frame into alignment, but with a frame well built good ribbands will greatly reduce the amount of dubbing. Ribbands should be fastened with ship spikes driven through washers or clinch rings, so that when the ribbands are pulled off the spikes will come with them.

HALF FRAMES AND CANTS

When the square-frames have been set up, the stem and main stern-frames are then erected and the keelsons and deadwood put down and fastened, after which the half frames or cants are set up, thus completing the frame.

Half frames and cants are assembled on small platforms to one side of the ship, and since they are in separate halves horning and half-breadth battens cannot be used. To assemble the lower tier to the proper shape, the timbers are placed on the platform in their proper order and shifted until they fit the mold from which they were marked out. This tier is dogged down, the butts cut in, and then refaired and dogged fast in the same manner as described for square-frames. The top tier is also handled in the same way as described for the top tier in square-frames.

To assist in placing half frames or cants, curved timbers called harpins are used. For the bow they extend from the stem to and past the last square-frame, as shown in Fig. 54. For the stern they will extend from the knuckle, rim, or last transom frame, as the case may be, to and past the last square-frame. In either case they follow the true shape of the vessel. Molds for these harpins are furnished from the loft and they are usually sawn to shape from straight grained timber.

At the bow harpins are usually set on a water-line, as shown in Fig. 54. At the stern they are set on a buttock line. Putting it another way, the harpins at the bow will curve in a horizontal direction only, while those at the stern will curve in a vertical direction only.

The frame centers should be marked on each harpin, as this will avoid the trouble of spacing around the curve of

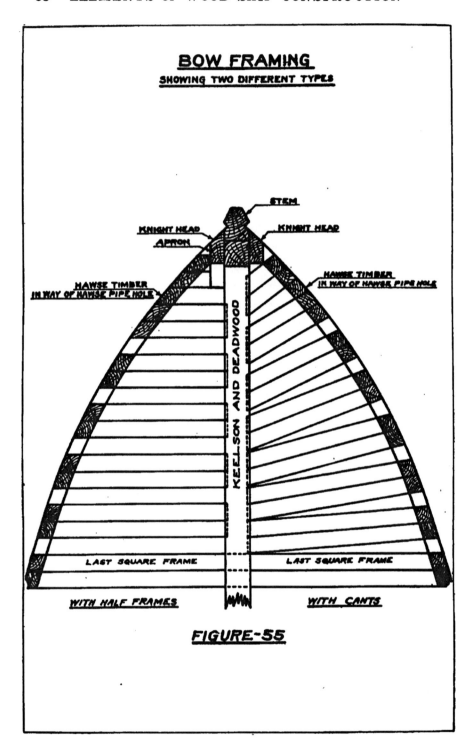

BOW FRAMING

SHOWING TWO DIFFERENT TYPES

STEM

KNIGHT HEAD

KNIGHT HEAD

APRON

HAWSE TIMBER
IN WAY OF HAWSE PIPE HOLE

HAWSE TIMBER
IN WAY OF HAWSE PIPE HOLE

KEELSON AND DEADWOOD

LAST SQUARE FRAME

LAST SQUARE FRAME

WITH HALF FRAMES

WITH CANTS

FIGURE-55

the bow and stern.   With the harpins in place, forming a cradle in which the half frame or cant may rest, the fitting of the heels of these frames remains as the only troublesome task.   In some yards where the heels are dapped into the deadwood, the mold is set up in the position of the frame after the dap has been cut and the heel of the mold corrected, after which the heel of the frame may be corrected very accurately before the frame is slung into position.   Even with this precaution, some refitting is very often necessary.

As soon as a pair of half frames or cants is in position they should be cross-pawled to take the weight off the harpins.   If this is delayed too long the weight of the frames will spring the harpins out of their true curve.   It is good practice to scribe the length of the cross-pawls from the loft at a stated height, then the frames can be brought to the marks on the cross-pawl and there is no danger of the spring of the harpin throwing the frame out of proper alignment.

For purposes of illustration, in Fig. 54 the harpins are shown on the 16-foot and 30-foot waterlines.   In practice they may be placed on any suitable waterline.   Harpins for the stern are not shown, as they involve precisely the same principles.

Figure 55 shows bow-framing of two types, cants, and half frames.   Cants are seldom used at the bow of steamers but are frequently used at the stern.   This figure also shows the knight-heads as usually fitted to a steamer.   The knight-heads here are fitted to fill out the bearding on the stem so as to obtain the proper room for the planking fastening.   They are molded from single timbers and fit solid against the apron and stem.   Knight-heads should be fastened with bolts driven through both knight-heads and apron and clinched on each end.

Where the anchor hawse pipes cut through the hull the space between the frames is filled solid with a timber extending some distance above and below the hole.   This timber, or there may be more than one, is called the hawse timber.   Fastening should be kept clear of the location

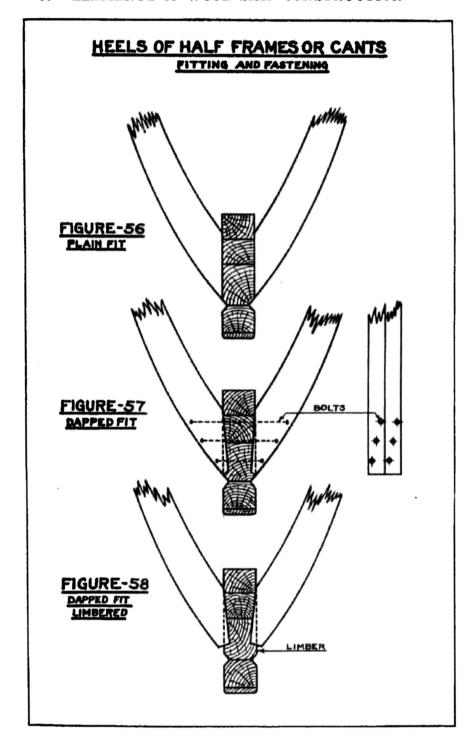

HEELS OF HALF FRAMES OR CANTS
FITTING AND FASTENING

FIGURE-56
PLAIN FIT

FIGURE-57
DAPPED FIT

BOLTS

FIGURE-58
DAPPED FIT
LIMBERED

LIMBER

for the hole. The procedure for hawse pipe holes also holds good for any opening to be cut in the bottom or sides of the hull and, before the planking or ceiling is put on, the spaces between frames in way of such opening should be chocked solid.

Heels of half frames or cants at the bow may be fitted to the deadwood in three different ways, as shown in Figs. 56, 57 and 58. The plain fit, shown in Fig. 56, is seldom used except in small vessels, and even for them it cannot be considered the best construction. The dapped fit, shown in Fig. 57, is most commonly used. However, the style shown in Fig. 58 has all of the advantages of the dapped fit, and the additional advantage of providing a limber for drainage at the ends of the vessel.

Heels of cants and half frames at the stern are fitted in the same manner as those at the bow, though structural arrangements may often prevent their being dapped in.

FRAME FASTENING

Immediately after a square-frame has been up-ended in its proper location on the keel a small drift-bolt is driven through the center of one of the floors into the keel to hold the frame in place. These frames receive their principal fastening when the keelson bolts are driven, as all of these, and there are at least four to the frame, pass through the floors and keel and are clinched on both ends.

On the other hand, half frames and cants must be fastened thoroughly when they are set up. Generally, all of the bolts fastening the heels of cants, or half frames, pass through the deadwood and opposite cant or half frame and are clinched on both ends. They may be arranged in location and number, as shown in Fig. 57, and it should be noted that the clinch rings, or heads, are counterbored well inside the face of the frame. This is done to get them well clear of the dubbing, which is very often quite heavy in this vicinity.

It is not always possible to drive through and clinch all of

TRANSOM FRAMES

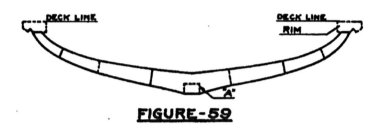

FIGURE-59

ARRANGEMENT OF FRAME FASTENINGS

FIGURE-60

LIMBERS

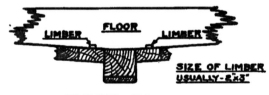

FIGURE-61

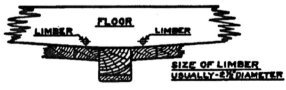

FIGURE-62

the heel fastening for cants, particularly stern cants, as will
be seen by referring to the radial stern cants shown in Fig.
65. The heels of these cants have plain fits, as shown in
Fig. 56, part of them being fitted against the last half frame
and the balance of them against what are called in this type
of stern, whisker timbers. In this case, to secure as much
through clinched fastening as possible, the erection would
begin at each end of the series of cants, and the last cant
placed in position would be the one landing in the crotch
between the last half frame and the whisker timber. Lack
of room would probably prevent through fastening the last
three cants erected, but this would be compensated for later
by placing a thwartship timber, called a transom, in way
of these cants and on top of the ceiling, which would be
clinch bolted through the cants before the planking is on.

There are an indefinite number of arrangements of stern
cants and half frames used, and it would be impossible even
briefly to describe all of them within the scope of these
chapters, but there are three principles which should apply
to all of them, which may be stated as follows: First, the
heels of all cants and half frames should be dapped at their
landings wherever possible; second, the heels should be
through clinch bolted wherever possible; third, where it is
impossible to through clinch bolt the heels of such cants or
half frames, compensation therefor should be provided
either by the fitting of transoms or other approved means.

LIMBERS

Limbers, unless of special type, must be cut in the floors
of all square-frames. If they are of the style shown in
Fig. 61, they should be cut as soon as the floors have been
sawn, and before the frames are assembled. If they are to
be as shown in Fig. 62, they should be bored as soon as
the frame is assembled on the framing stage. Either style
of limbers is generally arranged in a straight line along the
middle of the first garboard, as in this position the limbers
will clear the garboard fastening.

Limbers are usually fitted with $\frac{3}{8}''$ diameter close link galvanized chain, one length on each side of the keel, with the ends of the chains carried up through the ceiling and fastened.   Some slack is left so that the chain may be pulled back and forth to clear the limbers should they become clogged.   The chains should be lashed in place before the planking and ceiling are put on.   Then as soon as the garboard is in place the lashings are removed.

STERN-FRAMES

There are many styles of stern-frames, three of which, being typical, are shown in Figs. 63, 64, 65 and 66.   Figure 63 shows the center-line construction of a stern-frame that is almost universally used on small single deck western steamers, called steam schooners, and Fig. 64 shows the same frame completed.   This construction is peculiar in that from the propeller-post aft, the center-line timbers are so arranged that a series of transom frames may be fitted, thus securing great thwartship strength at this point. One of these transom frames is illustrated in Fig. 59.

These sterns are fitted with a rim, having a rabbet for the plank ends, and supported by the horn timbers and transom frames.   It will be noticed that the horn timbers extend over the top of the rim, to and against the solid work around the stern, thus affording an opportunity to drive several clinch bolts through rim and ends of the horn timbers.   The ceiling, when laid, is also carried up over the rim, where possible, to and against the solid work, and is well fastened into the rim.   The top of the rim is left flat and the decking, where the ceiling does not land in the way, is carried to the solid work and fastened into the rim. These vessels are fitted with a heavy fender or guard strake in line with the rim, this strake being scarfed to the forward ends of the latter, as shown in the figure.

The solid work around the stern extends to the first frame carried above the deck and carries all of the detail of the bulwark, rail, etc.   This feature will be more fully discussed later on.

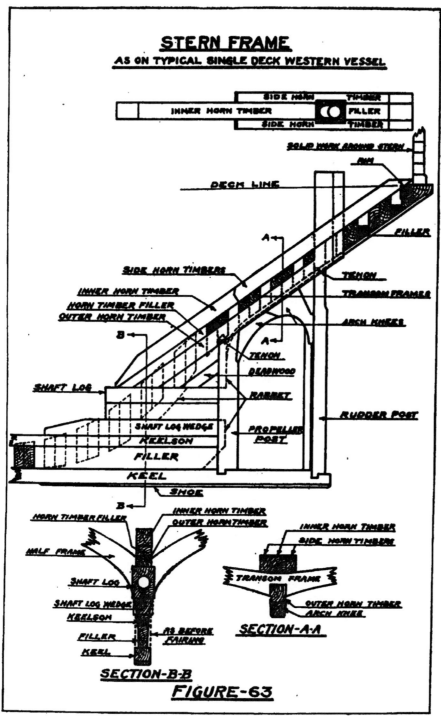

STERN FRAME

AS ON TYPICAL SINGLE DECK WESTERN VESSEL

FIGURE-63

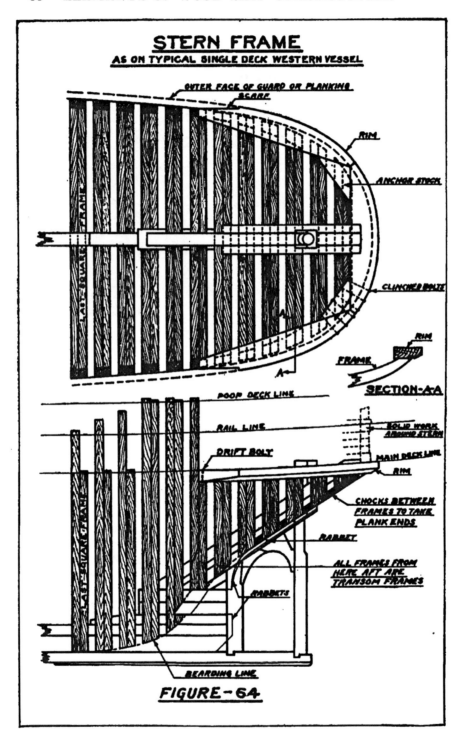

STERN FRAME

AS ON TYPICAL SINGLE DECK WESTERN VESSEL

OUTER FACE OF GUARD OR PLANKING
SCARF
RIM
ANCHOR STOCK
CLINCHER BOLTS

LAST SQUARE FRAME

A
A

RIM
FRAME
SECTION-A-A

POOP DECK LINE
RAIL LINE
DRIFT BOLT
SOLID WORK AROUND STERN
MAIN DECK LINE
RIM
CHOCKS BETWEEN FRAMES TO TAKE PLANK ENDS
RABBET
ALL FRAMES FROM HERE AFT ARE TRANSOM FRAMES

LAST SQUARE OF FRAME

RABBETS

BEARDING LINE

FIGURE-64

The poop erection on these vessels is often very short, and forward of same, in way of the bulwark, but one-half of the frame, that is, the stanchion, is carried above the deck, as shown in Fig. 64.

The figure shows the rudder trunk stopped at the main deck, but very often this is carried up to the poop deck. Other details may vary somewhat, according to the size of the vessel and the ideas of the builder, but in general the construction shown is typical, and forms a valuable basis of comparison with the other detail arrangements of sterns shown in Figs. 65 and 66. The latter types are at present being used on large vessels and while quite different in detail construction, both are considered good for the particular class of vessel in which they are used.

The center-line construction in Fig. 65, it will be seen, consists of a large propeller- or stern-post backed by the ends of the keelson, shaft-log, and deadwoods, and supporting by means of two very large natural crook knees, a false rudder-post, upon which, later, is mounted the bearing for a steel rudder. The rudder trunk is fitted and fastened to the after side of the false rudder-post. The lower knee is dapped into the propeller post at **B** to provide support in addition to that given by the fastenings.

On each side of this center-line detail, is placed a horn, or whisker timber, extending from the shaft-log to the knuckle. These timbers are slightly dapped into both the propeller and false rudder-posts. The space between them is filled solid with wood extending above their top edges, against which extension, later, the ceiling is butted. Aft of the false rudder-post this filler also extends below the edge of the whiskers to form a butt rabbet for the outside planking. Outside, a knuckle timber is fitted, carried around the stern until the side becomes straight enough to carry planking unbroken to the poop, or shelter, deck. The under side of this knuckle timber shows a rabbet for the lower hull planking. The planking above the knuckle runs parallel with the knuckle and the top face of the knuckle timber becomes, therefore, a seam.

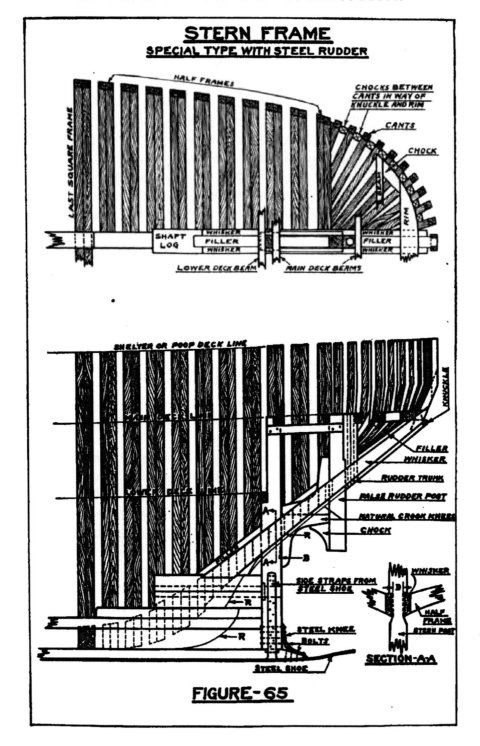

FIGURE-65

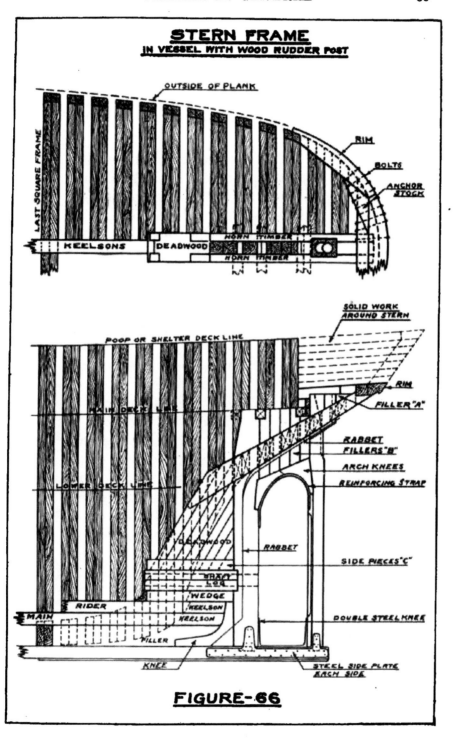

STERN FRAME
IN VESSEL WITH WOOD RUDDER POST

FIGURE-66

A small rim is fitted inside the cants with its top face on the deck line, to receive the ends of the decking.

It will be noticed that the cants and half frames land on the whiskers, and that they are so molded that the planking will land on and fasten to the outer face of the timbers, while the ceiling will land on and fasten to the inner face of the timbers.

A steel knee is fitted at the lower end of the propeller-post onto the keel, and on the under side of the keel a steel shoe is fitted, with long side straps extending up each side of the propeller-post, the shoe also extending aft to carry the lower bearing of the steel rudder. The side straps of the shoe are clinch bolted to each other through the propeller-post. The lower leg of the knee is clinch bolted to the shoe through the end of the keel, and the upper leg is bolted through the propeller-post with bolts having nuts on each end, the nuts on the forward end being mortised in. These mortises are afterwards filled with cement. The extension of the shoe along the keel is also well fastened with heavy drift bolts.

Detail arrangement of fastening for the center-line timbers of this stern is shown in Fig. 67.

Figure 66 shows a center-line detail consisting of a large propeller, or stern-post, backed on the forward side by the ends of the keelsons, shaft-log, and deadwoods, and joined to the keel by a natural crook wood knee. Aft of the propeller-post is a full wood rudder-post stepped to the end of the keel, and the space between the upper ends of the two posts is filled solid with vertically disposed deadwood fillers, flush with the siding of the posts. Arch knees are fitted across the lower ends of these fillers to finish off and strengthen the construction. On each side of the upper ends of the posts there is a horn timber extending aft to, and supporting, the rim, which is here placed some distance above the deck line. Between the forward ends of the horn timbers there are several tiers of deadwood extending to the shaft-log, the lower ends fitting between the side pieces C, which are placed on top of the log at each side. The tops

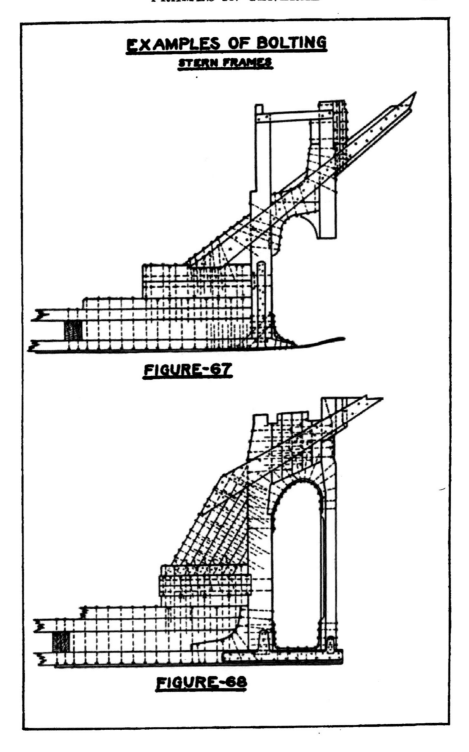

EXAMPLES OF BOLTING

STERN FRAMES

FIGURE-67

FIGURE-68

of the propeller-post and fillers show cuts in way of deck beams so that they may be carried through from side to side in one piece. The sterns of these vessels above the rim are generally built up of solid work, as indicated in the figure. Some have been built with radial frames extending up from the rim and mortised into the same, but this construction is somewhat weaker than that obtained with the solid work.

The lower face of the arch knees is lined with a steel reinforcing strap extending down on each post and well fastened.

Side plates of steel are fitted on each side of the keel, with arms extending up on the propeller- and rudder-posts. These plates are fastened to each other through the keel and posts with clinched bolts.

Fastening for this type of stern is shown in detail in Fig. 68. Details for this and other fastening discussed here, are usually shown on the plans of the ship, which may vary considerably in detail arrangement from that shown in these figures. Sizes of bolts are not indicated in the figure, as they vary with the sizes of the timbers and the requirements of the Classification Society under which the vessel is being built.

GLOSSARY

Bevel—A term used to indicate that one side of a timber is not square with another side. Bevels in ship work are referred to as "standing" or "under." See Fig. 72. Bevels are indicated from the molding, or laying out face of the timber, and from this face a standing bevel will be outsquare, and an underbevel insquare.

Bilge—The sharp turn of the frame between the floor and the straight side. A term used in referring to details located in the vicinity of the bilge, as "bilge ceiling," "bilge shores," "bilge plank," etc.

Bilge Water—Water inside the hull of a ship gained through leakage.

Cant—A half frame which has been swung out of square with the center line of the ship. Forward cants would be swung in a forward direction, and after cants would be swung aft. To cant means to swing, or lean.

Deadrise—The slope of the under part of the floor on the midship frame, which is straight, that is, that part of the floor between the keel and the beginning of the turn of the bilge. Deadrise may be stated in terms of inches to the foot, or it may be given as so many inches in the half breadth of the ship. For instance, in a vessel having a beam of 44

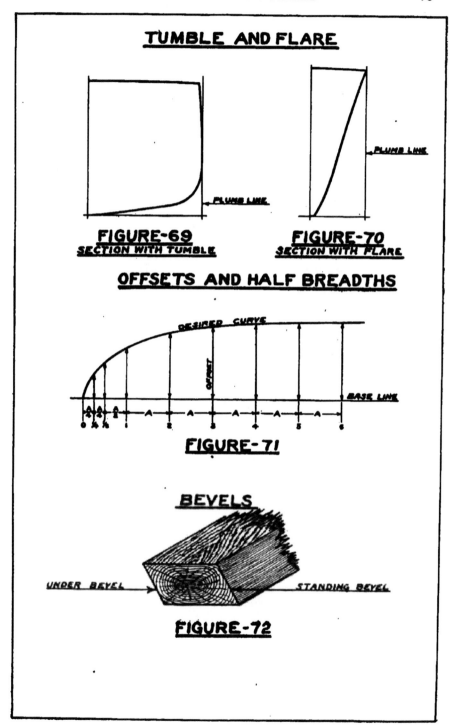

TUMBLE AND FLARE

FIGURE-69
SECTION WITH TUMBLE

FIGURE-70
SECTION WITH FLARE

OFFSETS AND HALF BREADTHS

FIGURE-71

BEVELS

FIGURE-72

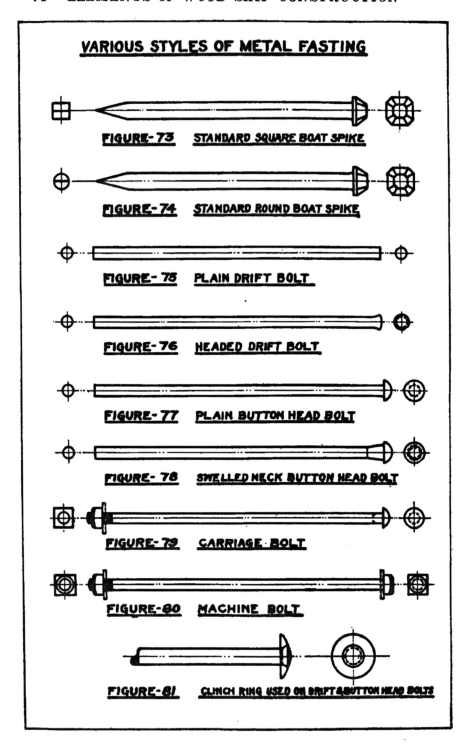

VARIOUS STYLES OF METAL FASTING

FIGURE-73   STANDARD SQUARE BOAT SPIKE

FIGURE-74   STANDARD ROUND BOAT SPIKE

FIGURE-75   PLAIN DRIFT BOLT

FIGURE-76   HEADED DRIFT BOLT

FIGURE-77   PLAIN BUTTON HEAD BOLT

FIGURE-78   SWELLED NECK BUTTON HEAD BOLT

FIGURE-79   CARRIAGE BOLT

FIGURE-80   MACHINE BOLT

FIGURE-81   CLINCH RING USED ON DRIFT & BUTTON HEAD BOLTS

feet, the half beam would be 22 feet. If the deadrise was given as a total of 11 inches, the slope would be ½ inch to the foot. The total deadrise would be measured where a straight line, extended from the flat of the floor, would intersect a plumb-line drawn down from the side of the ship at the deck line.

Deadwood—Timbers and fillers along the center line of the ship, to fill in between ends of keelson and keel, and on top of keelsons forward, or on top of shaftlog aft.

Fastening—A general term applied to nails, spikes, bolts and treenails, used in fastening up a ship. Various kinds of metal fastening used in the hull are shown in Figs. 73 to 81, inclusive.

Flare—A term used in describing a section of the ship having the general shape shown in Fig. 70.

Half-breadth—One-half the breadth through the vessel at any given point. One-half the total breadth of any figure symmetrical about a base line. If the curve in Fig. 71 was extended on both sides of the base line and was the same on each side, the distances marked offsets would then be half-breadths. Half-breadths may be taken at regular intervals in the same manner as offsets.

Half Frame—Any frame set square with the center line of the ship, but which does not cross the keel.

Limbers—Small openings or channels cut in the floors of frames, or on other timbers, to permit drainage of the bilge water to the pump suctions.

Offsets—The distances at regular or irregular intervals from a straight line, called the base, to a curve. Offsets are ordinarily taken at regular intervals and if it should be necessary to close space them at any point they are spaced at some even fraction of the common interval. See Fig. 71.

Parallel Body—That portion of the ship amidships, where all of the frames are of the same size and without bevel.

Square Frame—Any frame in a vessel which crosses the keel and is fitted with floor timbers.

Tumble—A term used to describe the form of a ship's section, such as shown in Fig. 69.

FOREWORD TO CHAPTER III

Mention has already been made of the order in which the keelsons and frames are placed in the ship, and of the fact that the ship's frame is in reality not completed until the main keelsons are down. From this point of progress the usual order of procedure would be about as follows: First, the dubbers are started to work on the inside of the frame. Ordinarily this work may be started as soon as enough of the square frames are up to permit ribbanding. In any event the dubbing should be kept well in advance of the ceiling gangs.

Following up the dubbing, the first timbers to be placed, after the frame is completed are generally the sister keelsons. Then the heavy ceiling is started, the lowermost strake at the lower turn of the bilge being the first put down. Where the ceiling is not edge bolted two gangs may be worked, and the ceiling would be started off in two places, first at the lowermost heavy bilge strake as above, and again at some point between decks, both gangs working from starting point upwards.

Where the ceiling is edge bolted, and it is the general rule to use edge bolts, then the operation of ceiling must begin with the lowermost strake that is edge bolted, which is generally the lowest heavy bilge strake, and continue in order thence to the uppermost clamp, the edge bolts being driven in each strake as it is run in. Deck beams below the upper deck must be placed as soon as the ceiling gang reaches the deck line. Likewise as soon as the deck beams are in, any waterways occurring on that deck must be run in before the ceiling can be carried upward. The running in of the waterways usually calls for the fitting of the shelves, in fact it is usually wise to fit both of these items at the same time as the fastening then can be driven to better advantage. Before the shelves and waterways are fitted however, the deck beams must first have been sprung to the proper camber. Beams below the upper deck are not usually cambered. If there are no shelves, and hanging knees are to be fitted they may be placed as soon as the beams have been pumped up to their camber. During this time the hold stanchions may also be fitted and ironed up.

There is no set time for the placing of the thin bottom ceiling and it may be run in any time after the lower heavy bilge strake has been placed. It is often the last ceiling to be placed. However it should all be in place before any of the planking is started.

NOTE.—Although waterways are mentioned in this chapter it is considered that they more properly belong under the heading of deck details and they will therefore not be fully described until the next chapter.

It is most convenient to construct the lower hold bulkheads before the decking is laid, although bulkheads between decks are not generally built until after the deck upon which they rest has been laid. The arrangement shown in the detail plans will indicate the best order of procedure.

Pointers, if fitted to the ship, should be placed immediately after the ceiling, deck beams, and shelves are up.

Tabulation of the Order of Procedure Inboard Hull Details

MAIN OPERATION	COINCIDENT OPERATION
Dubbing.	
Laying of sister keelsons.	Dubbing.
Fitting thick ceiling at bilge.	Dubbing.
Fitting lower deck clamps.	
Setting lower deck beams.	
Fitting shelves and waterways (lower deck).	Setting lower hold stanchions.
Fitting tween deck ceiling.	
Fitting upper deck clamps.	Laying thin ceiling (bottom).
Setting upper deck beams.	
Fitting shelves and waterways (upper deck).	Setting tween deck stanchions.
Fitting lower hold bulkheads.	Fitting pointers.

This tabulation is arranged for a ship having two decks, it also being assumed that the ceiling is edge bolted.

CHAPTER III

INBOARD HULL DETAILS .

KEELSONS

The number and arrangement of keelson strakes appears to be within certain limits purely a matter of individual taste with the designer. There is apparently but a vague relation between the size of the ship and either the number or sizes of the keelsons employed. The number of individual arrangements used is much too large to even attempt to describe within the scope of these chapters. The types shown in Figs. 82 to 85 inclusive are types that have been used quite recently and therefore may be said to be of interest as indicating present-day ideas. The size of the ship, as well as the sizes of each of the keelson strakes employed in each type, are set down, so that the reader may be better able to follow the slight relation which does exist between the different types and the sizes of the vessels in which they have been used.

Type No. I, Fig. 82, it will be noted, consists of a main keelson with two strakes of rider keelsons above it, and one sister keelson on each side. Type II, Fig. 83, consists of a main keelson with five strakes of sister keelsons on each side of it. Type No. III, Fig. 84, consists of a main keelson with one rider, and a sister keelson on each side, each sister keelson having one rider making a six-strake keelson set. Included in this system are the girder keelsons, some distance out each side of the centerline keelsons. Each girder keelson consists of a lower strake locked over the floors and two lighter riders.

Inasmuch as the keelsons in this figure are used in large vessels as are also the ones shown in the figure following, which are very much lighter, it has been deemed best to

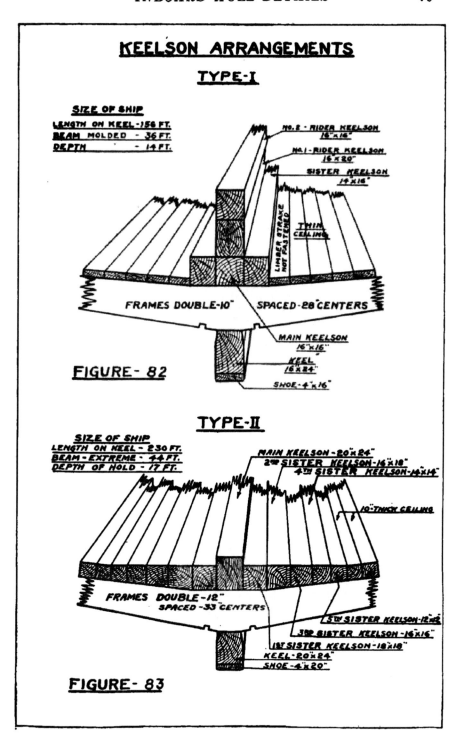

KEELSON ARRANGEMENTS

TYPE-I

SIZE OF SHIP
LENGTH ON KEEL - 156 FT.
BEAM MOLDED - 36 FT.
DEPTH - 14 FT.

NO.2 - RIDER KEELSON 16"x16"
NO.1 - RIDER KEELSON 16"x20"
SISTER KEELSON 14"x16"
THIN CEILING
LIMBER STRAKE NOT FASTENED

FRAMES DOUBLE-10" SPACED-28" CENTERS

MAIN KEELSON 16"x16"
KEEL 16"x24"
SHOE-4"x16"

FIGURE-82

TYPE-II

SIZE OF SHIP
LENGTH ON KEEL - 230 FT.
BEAM - EXTREME - 44 FT.
DEPTH OF HOLD - 17 FT.

MAIN KEELSON-20"x24"
2ND SISTER KEELSON-16"x18"
4TH SISTER KEELSON-14"x14"
10"-THICK CEILING

FRAMES DOUBLE-12" SPACED-33" CENTERS

5TH SISTER KEELSON-12"x12"
3RD SISTER KEELSON-16"x16"
1ST SISTER KEELSON-18"x18"
KEEL-20"x24"
SHOE-4"x20"

FIGURE-83

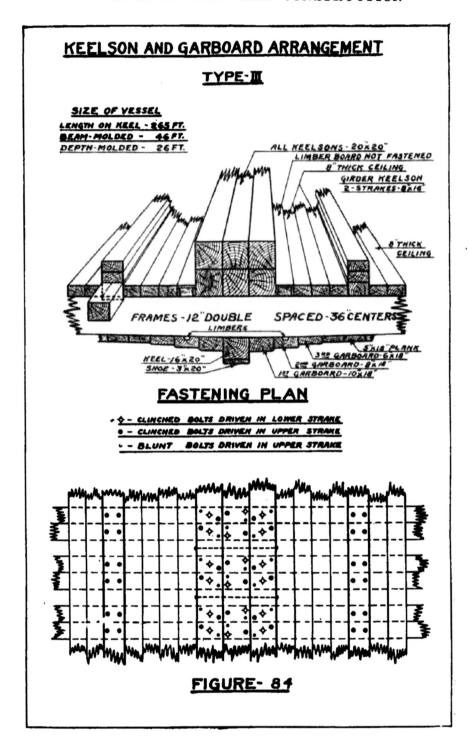

KEELSON AND GARBOARD ARRANGEMENT

TYPE-III

SIZE OF VESSEL
LENGTH ON KEEL - 265 FT.
BEAM - MOLDED - 46 FT.
DEPTH - MOLDED - 26 FT.

ALL KEELSONS - 20"x20"
LIMBER BOARD NOT FASTENED
8" THICK CEILING
GIRDER KEELSON
2 - STRAKES - 8x16

8" THICK CEILING

FRAMES - 12" DOUBLE   SPACED - 36" CENTERS
LIMBERS

KEEL - 16"x20"
SHOE - 3"x20"

5"x18" PLANK
3RD GARBOARD - 6x18
2ND GARBOARD - 8x18
1ST GARBOARD - 10x18

FASTENING PLAN

⬦ - CLINCHED BOLTS DRIVEN IN LOWER STRAKE
● - CLINCHED BOLTS DRIVEN IN UPPER STRAKE
└ - BLUNT BOLTS DRIVEN IN UPPER STRAKE

FIGURE - 84

show at this point, the keel, and planking arrangement next to it, for each of the types so that a more comprehensive idea of the actual relative centerline strength may be had. As a matter of interest, note that the limbers in Fig. 84 are cut along the center of the second garboard strake, and not in the frames. This arrangement, up to the time of its use in these vessels, was not a common one except in yachts and smaller vessels. However it is a good one, wherever it can be used, as it avoids cutting and weakening the floor at this point. Obviously this style of limber could not be used in Fig. 85.

In Type IV, Fig. 85, it will be noted that there are but three strakes of keelsons. The outside planking is laid over two courses of thinner diagonal planking. These courses of diagonal planking cover the entire frame of the vessel. The lower ends, it will be seen in the figure, butt against the keel, the chocks marked "B" being fitted in the frame bays to receive the end fastening at those points.

In Fig. 84 there is no diagonal planking. In its place there is what is known as diagonal strapping, that is iron straps extending from the upper deck line down around the bilge to the floor heads, all arranged in both directions diagonally. This will be more fully described in the following chapters.

Essentially the arrangement shown in Fig. 84 belongs to the heavy scantling class of vessel, while that shown in Fig. 85 belongs to the light scantling class. This accounts for the principal differences in the two arrangements although some allowance may have possibly been made for the fact that diagonal planking is by many authorities considered more efficient than the strapping.

The fastening plans for each of these styles of keelsons are shown at the bottom of the plates and are self-explanatory. In both figures all clinched bolts driven in the main keelson, or its rider, are put through the keel and headed up over rings below. In Fig. 84 the sister keelson clinched bolts pass through the floors only while in Fig. 85 they pass through the first garboard and are headed up over rings

6

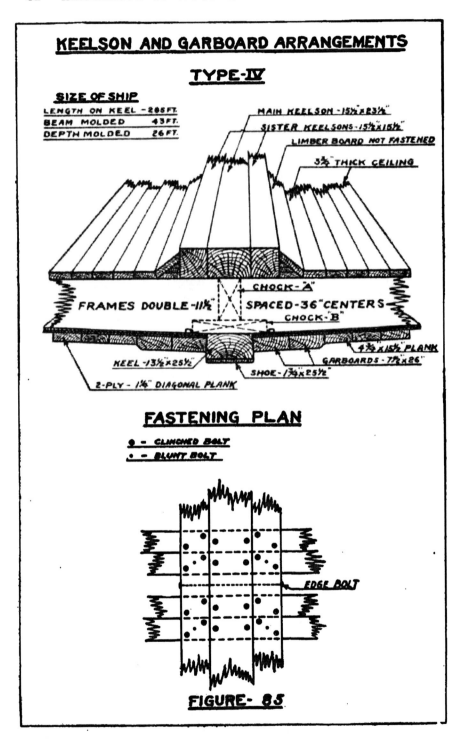

KEELSON AND GARBOARD ARRANGEMENTS

TYPE-IV

SIZE OF SHIP
LENGTH ON KEEL - 285 FT.
BEAM MOLDED   43 FT.
DEPTH MOLDED   26 FT.

MAIN KEELSON - 15½ x 23½"
SISTER KEELSONS - 15½ x 15½"
LIMBER BOARD NOT FASTENED
3½" THICK CEILING

CHOCK-"A"
FRAMES DOUBLE - 11½   SPACED-36"CENTERS
CHOCK-"B"

4⅜ x 15½ PLANK
KEEL - 13½ x 25½   GARBOARDS - 7⅞ x 26"
SHOE - 1¾ x 25½"
2-PLY - 1¼" DIAGONAL PLANK

FASTENING PLAN

● - CLINCHED BOLT
· - BLUNT BOLT

EDGE BOLT

FIGURE- 85

below. In both systems the sister keelsons are edge bolted, it being generally customary to drive the bolts through and clinch them. Their number and arrangement may vary somewhat in different vessels, as also may the other fastening. In all cases detail plans are furnished, showing the exact arrangement of the fastening, and should be carefully followed.

KEELSON SCARFS

Keelson scarfs are proportioned by the same rules that already have been given for keel scarfs. However, the lower nib, when falling against a floor where it is concealed, is frequently made only one inch deep instead of the rule depth of possibly several times this. The locations of the various scarfs are usually shown on the plans. They should be arranged so as to use the longest available timbers and should be properly shifted in the various strakes. No fixed rule can be given for the shifting of keelson scarfs. They should be kept as far apart as possible and in no case should any part of a scarf in one strake overlap any part of a scarf in another strake unless the number of keelson strakes is greater than eight. Scarfs in adjoining strakes should have from six to eight frame bays between them if possible.

All keelson scarfs are commonly made flat, that is, with the flat of the nib resting on the floors, or keelson strake underneath. It is common to speak of keelson scarfs as flat when they are in this position, even where occurring in a keelson having greater molding than siding, when, according to rule, the scarf would be an edge scarf. It is good practice to so face the scarfs as to permit the placing of the midship lengths of the main keelson first, thus permitting this work to be done as soon as enough of the square frames are up to receive a full timber length. There will then be no time lost in getting the main keelson ends down after the square frame has been completed.

The sister keelsons are generally run in beginning at the bow and working to the stern. The ends of the sister

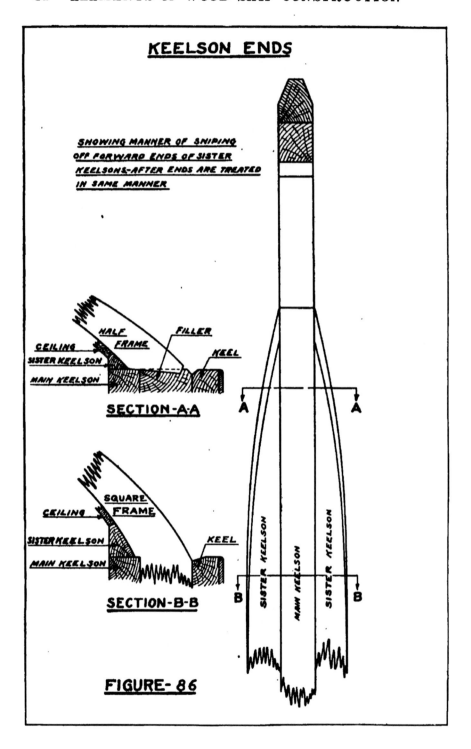

KEELSON ENDS

SHOWING MANNER OF SNIPING OFF FORWARD ENDS OF SISTER KEELSONS-AFTER ENDS ARE TREATED IN SAME MANNER

SECTION-A-A

SECTION-B-B

FIGURE-86

keelsons forward and aft are sniped off to fay to the edges of the ceiling coming in contact with them at that point. This is accomplished in the manner shown in Fig. 86. The ends of the sister keelsons may be worked out from offsets furnished from the loft, these being carefully checked from the ship before cutting the timbers to exact size.

Where there is more than one set of sister keelsons, as in Fig. 83, each keelson strake would be run straight fore and aft, or parallel with the keel, and the ceiling would run across the ends of the keelsons as indicated for the one strake in Fig. 86. Thus it will be noted that, before the final shape of the ends of assistant keelsons can be laid out, the ceiling line crossing them must be run in. This line is sometimes that of the lower edge of the thick bilge ceiling as is described further on in this chapter.

In some cases the sister keelsons are cut off square a short distance from their natural endings, and "thick strakes" are fitted, these being about the same shape as the keelson ends would have been if extended as shown in the figure. These short timbers are easier to handle and fit, and that is the principal object in using them.

CLAMPS AND SHELVES

In general, there are three arrangements of clamps and shelves in common use. First, as shown in Figs. 87 to 89 inclusive, we have clamps only, an arrangement that may be used only where a hanging knee is fitted under each beam. Second, in Fig. 90, we have an arrangement of light shelves and clamps, in combination with hanging knees, the latter being fitted under approximately every other beam. Third, and last, we have the heavy shelf and clamp arrangement shown in Fig. 91, in which there are no hanging knees.

Fastening arrangements which have been used are shown in each figure and are self-explanatory. It will be noted that in all types except Fig. 91 the fastenings are driven in the middle of the frame timber. The arrangement

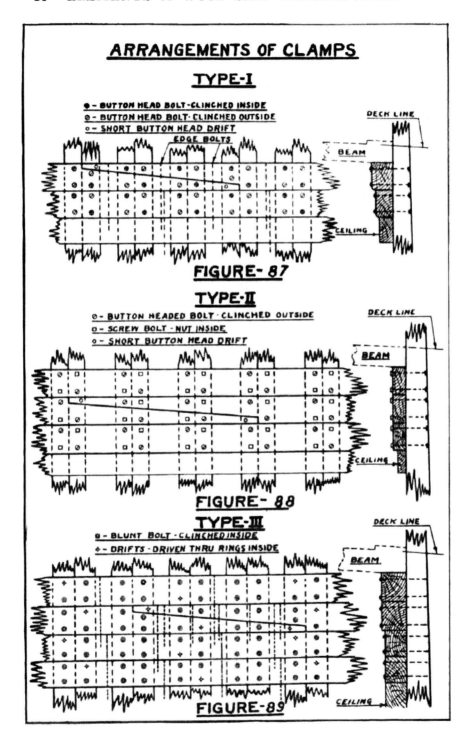

ARRANGEMENTS OF CLAMPS

TYPE-I

FIGURE- 87

TYPE-II

FIGURE- 88

TYPE-III

FIGURE-89

in Fig. 91 is an unusual one. The space between the center of the timber and the side is generally reserved for planking fastening much of which has to be driven through frame and ceiling. Where both systems are ranged on the same line it makes it very difficult to get the planking fastening through without striking iron.

CLAMP AND SHELF SCARFS

Clamp strakes should be of the longest possible length and scarfed strictly according to rule, that is, insofar as the length of the scarf is concerned. Where the rule lengths do not land the nibs on the frames properly the length should be increased, not decreased.

Scarfs in clamps may be either flat or edge scarfs, and if made flat there should be very little if any reduction in length under that required for the edge scarf. Modern practice leans somewhat toward the flat scarf as all of the main fastenings then pass through both parts of the scarf, while in an edge scarf the edge bolting constitutes the only direct connection between the two parts. Edge scarfs should have standard nibs. Flat scarfs should have the inboard nib of standard depth, while the outboard nib, which should always rest against a frame, may be from one inch in depth to a feathered edge. The cutting of any outboard nib at all in a flat scarf makes the fitting of the scarf very difficult, and inasmuch as the outboard nib is supported by the frame it may just as well be feathered off, in which case the fitting of the inboard nib and the scarf becomes a very simple and ordinary operation.

All scarfs in shelves should have standard nibs. Assuming that the least dimension of the shelf strakes is the molded, or vertical, dimension, the scarfs would ordinarily be edge scarfs and would have extra edge bolting as driven in clamp edge scarfs.

As has already been mentioned, the clamps should be of the longest available timbers, and it follows that the scarfs should be well shifted. In determining the proper shift of scarfs in the clamps it is necessary to consider also the shelves and waterways as they are also important strength members of the same group.   There should be no overlap of scarfs unless there are more than a total of eight strakes in the entire system of shelves, clamps and waterways.   Scarfs in adjoining strakes should have from six to eight frames spaces between them wherever possible.

To follow out the above rules strictly requires very long timbers, which, in some localities are not available. The plans for the vessel generally take into account the available lengths of timbers and therefore considerable variation from the rules stated here may be found in practice.

CLAMP AND SHELF FASTENINGS

Practice in the method of driving clamp and shelf fastening varies considerable, although the number of fastenings to the frame is rather uniform.   For instance, in Fig. 87 there are four fastenings to the frame, two button head bolts driven from the inside and clinched outside, and two driven from the outside and clinched inside.   This is a rather unusual fastening.   In Fig. 88 there are again four fastenings to the frame, two of them being button headed bolts driven from the inside and clinched outside, and two machine bolts with nuts inside. This is also a rather unusual fastening.   In Fig. 89 there are still four fastenings to the frame all of which except one working fastening per frame are headed blunt bolts driven from the outside and clinched inside.   The working fastening consists of drift bolts driven through rings inside.   In Fig. 90 there are four fastenings to the frame two of which are button-headed bolts driven from the outside and clinched inside and two button headed bolts driven from the inside to within about one inch of the outside of the frame.   Note that some of the fastening is omitted in way of the knee.   The number of fastenings that may be omitted in way of hanging knees is governed by the amount of knee fastening to be driven.   For instance

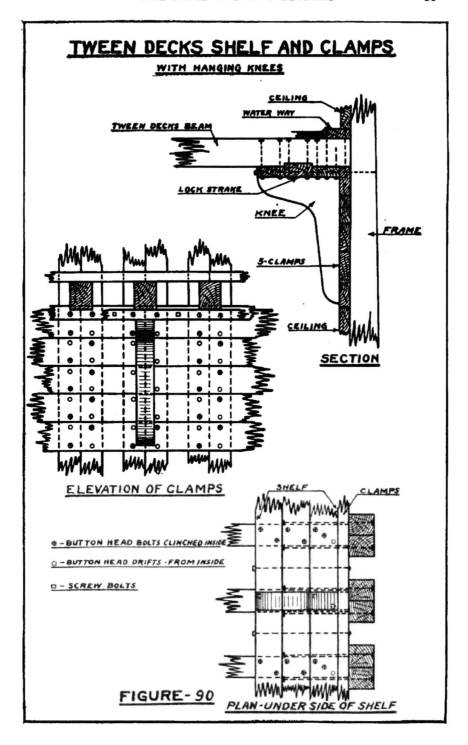

TWEEN DECKS SHELF AND CLAMPS
WITH HANGING KNEES

CEILING
WATER WAY
TWEEN DECKS BEAM
LOCK STRAKE
KNEE
FRAME
S-CLAMPS
CEILING

SECTION

ELEVATION OF CLAMPS

● - BUTTON HEAD BOLTS CLINCHED INSIDE

○ - BUTTON HEAD DRIFTS - FROM INSIDE

□ - SCREW BOLTS

SHELF
CLAMPS

FIGURE - 90

PLAN - UNDER SIDE OF SHELF

if the lower leg of the knee in Fig. 90 had eight through fastenings, then it would be possible to omit that number of fastenings from the clamps in way of the knee.

Likewise if four of the knee bolts are clinched bolts, then four of the bolts omitted from the clamps may be clinched bolts. Obviously this rule must be applied with some judgment to avoid leaving out too much fastening in in one place and bunching it in another.

In Fig. 91 all of the bolts fastening the clamps and shelves to the frame are headed blunt bolts driven from the outside. Of course a few of these bolts must be driven from the inside as working fastening but this number is held to a minimum. All of the fastening must be set well in on the outside of the frame to clear the dubbing. Button-headed bolts driven from the outside should be set down in counterbores. Headed drifts, or blunt bolts, may be set in without counterboring.

Clamps, like the ceiling, which will be described later, are generally edge bolted. The customary arrangement is one bolt passing through two and one-half strakes driven in each strake in alternate frame bays, but in many instances bolts of the same length are driven in each frame bay for at least a portion of the length of the ship. Edge scarfs should receive extra edge bolts sufficient to bring the total number of such bolts up to not less than two to the frame bay. Quite frequently more are driven. The same rule for extra edge bolting also applies to scarfs in the shelves.

The fact has already been mentioned that it is desirable to run in the shelf and waterway strakes practically simultaneously. This is principally due to the necessary arrangement of fastening. For instance referring to Fig. 90 it will be seen that it would be advisable to run in the first strake of the shelf and then the waterway, before proceeding with the other strakes of the shelf. When this is done the work can be fastened as it goes along which always makes the better job. Again, referring to Fig. 91 it will be seen that the waterway fastening passes through the shelf

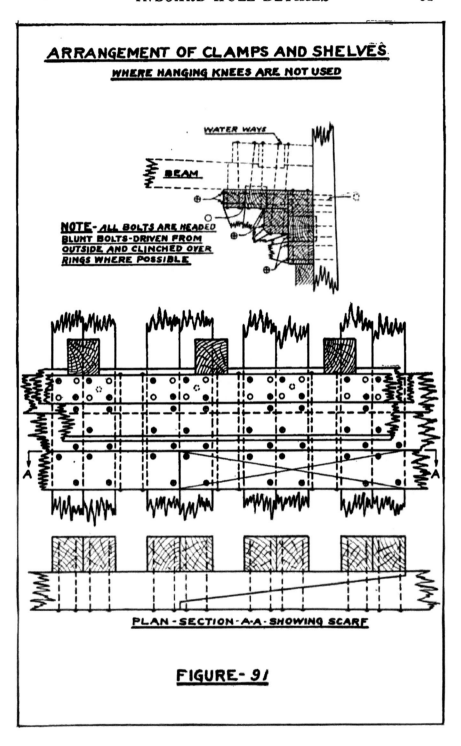

ARRANGEMENT OF CLAMPS AND SHELVES

WHERE HANGING KNEES ARE NOT USED

WATER WAYS

BEAM

NOTE- *ALL BOLTS ARE HEADED BLUNT BOLTS-DRIVEN FROM OUTSIDE AND CLINCHED OVER RINGS WHERE POSSIBLE*

A

A

PLAN - SECTION - A·A · SHOWING SCARF

FIGURE- 91

and is clinched below. The shelves are also fastened horizontally into the frame, as are also the waterways, although the bolts are not shown in this figure. It will be readily seen that in order to secure the best job the waterways and shelves should be run in at the same time so the fastening each way in each strake can all be driven, thus securing and holding the strake "home."

MISCELLANEOUS

Toward the ends of the vessel the curvature becomes so sharp that it is often impossible to spring the shelf strakes into place and they must therefore be worked out to shape. This is especially true where shelves are carried around elliptical sterns. Very often the shelf strakes are not carried to the extreme ends of the ship. Forward they may be allowed to stop at the collision bulkhead, aft they may be allowed to butt against an inside rim. As a matter of good design, while they may be reduced in size at the ends of the ship, all shelf and clamp strakes should be carried as far forward and aft as possible. Tapering such heavy strakes as the shelves and clamps shown in Fig. 91, as they near the ends of the ship, is not only good practice but serves a very useful purpose. Such strakes if untapered are almost impossible to spring around the luff of the bow in good shape. In the majority of cases they would be split by the band saw before attempting to spring them into place. The latter operation merely converts the timber into two thinner timbers thus making it easier to bend. Tapering serves the same purpose and has the additional advantage of saving some timber and weight.

CEILING

Heavy scantling ceiling is shown in Fig. 92. Light scantling ceiling is shown in Fig. 93. Since the two figures are the same size and were originally drawn to the same scale, the relative proportions of the ceilings are approxi-

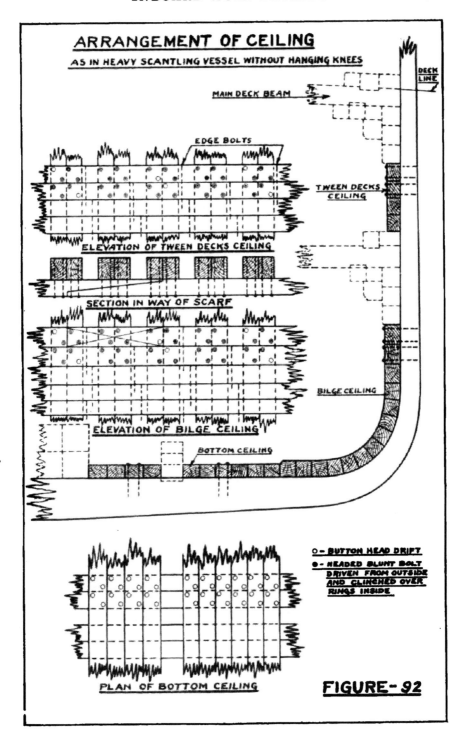

FIGURE-92

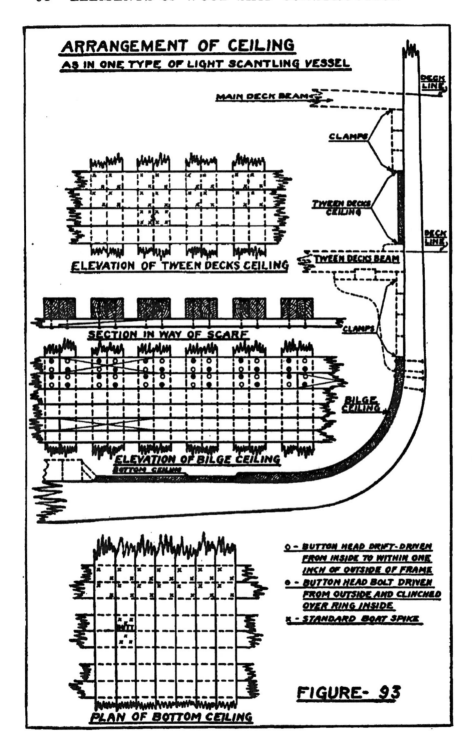

FIGURE- 93

mately true and afford a very interesting comparison between the two types of construction. :

The operation of ceiling properly begins with the lowermost strake of the heavy, or bilge, ceiling, although as has been previously mentioned, in a vessel having the cross section shown in Fig. 93, where there are no edge bolts in the ceiling, the work may be started at both the lower edge of the bilge ceiling and at some point between decks. The latter arrangement is the exception to the general rule.

CEILING LINING

The lining of the ceiling is a very simple operation though requiring some skill and experience to obtain a result pleasing to the eye.

The first line to be established in the lining operation is that of the upper deck. The points indicating the location of this line, it will be remembered are marked on the top timbers, or stanchions, when the frame is molded, but as the frame has gone through the process of assembling and erecting since these points were marked, they could hardly be expected to remain at exactly their proper height or in a fair line. Therefore fairing, or sheer, battens must be tacked up on each side of the ship, care being taken to so place the battens that they will be at the proper height above the top of the keel at all points. It will be found generally that the points previously marked on the frames will have to be disregarded, but they will still form a valuable guide for setting the battens. The proper heights for the battens should be entirely remeasured at a sufficient number of points to insure their proper location, after which they may be faired between these points by the eye. In general the old deck-line points will be found below the true points, due to natural settling of the frame, and to the shifting down of the timbers when the butts are cut in on the framing stage.

In some yards the sheer battens are placed on the outside of the hull, but in most cases it will be found best to place them on the inside of the frames, as in this position the eye can follow them from end to end of the ship.

Once this line is established, the tweendecks line, or any deck line below the upper deck line, may be lined out by simply measuring down the proper distance from the upper deck line. These distances are always shown on the detail plans.

The line of the lower strake of the heavy bilge ceiling is determined by two conditions: First, the permissible am ount of taper in the siding of the bilge strakes at the ends of the ship, and second, the position of the line should be such as to permit running all strakes without spiling, *i. e.*, it should be possible to edge set all strakes into place.

The first condition is merely a matter of measurement down from the lowest deck line, the distances first measured being such as will allow a reasonable amount of taper on the hoods. This will approximately establish the line of the lower bilge strake. Then, to find out if the second condition is satisfied a thin batten is set along this line, the batten being allowed to "fly" at the forward and after ends of the ship. The amount it springs above the line will indicate the amount of edge set required to get the strake into place. An experienced liner's judgment will at once tell him if it is possible.

If, after this line is run in, the thick ceiling does not extend down far enough to cross the assistant keelson ends, then strakes of the thin ceiling are carried around on the ceiling line to close off this work. The balance of the thin ceiling is run straight fore and aft, the ends being nibbed into the adjoining strakes in much the same manner as will later be described for decking.

Once the deck lines have been established, and the lower line run in, the work of lining the ceiling then becomes merely a matter of fitting a given number of strakes in a given room. By spacing off the number of strakes, at frequent intervals into the total room to be occupied by them the width of each strake at each interval is obtained. Then all of the strakes for that particular room will be cut the same widths and tapers. This operation will be more fully described under "Planking."

The most important single operation in ceiling, with the possible exception of the lining, is the bevel taking. There are two general methods of beveling so that the edges will fit together. The first, shown in Fig. 94, can be used in any location. Here both edges of each strake are beveled off, each bevel being about the same. The second method shown in Fig. 95 is where only one edge of the ceiling is beveled, the other edge being left square. It will be seen that where the bevels are heavy, as around the bilge the latter method leaves projecting corners inside. Therefore the second system should not be used where the bevels are very heavy.

The total equipment for bevel taking consists of a ship carpenter's bevel, a bevel board, Fig. 96, and a degree board, Fig. 97. Only one edge of the bevel board need be straight.

With these tools at hand the bevel taking would proceed much as follows: First, the bevel would be held in the position shown in Fig. 94, the handle being held firmly against the edge of the strake in place, the blade being so set as to give the correct bevel for the next strake. This will require some practice as will be seen from the following explanation.

If the length of the bevel blade was exactly the same as the width of the strake for which the bevel was being taken then the correct bevel would be obtained by setting the blade hard against the frame. As a rule, however, the bevel blade is shorter than the width of the strake, so the blade should not be set hard against the frame but should be set in the position it would assume, if its length were the same as the width of the strake and it had been set hard against the frame. Thus it will be seen, that, where the bevel blade is short, it will set out from the frame at the upper end, when adjusted to the proper bevel. The amount of this "set out" must be determined by experience.

Second, the bevels thus obtained are transferred to the

7

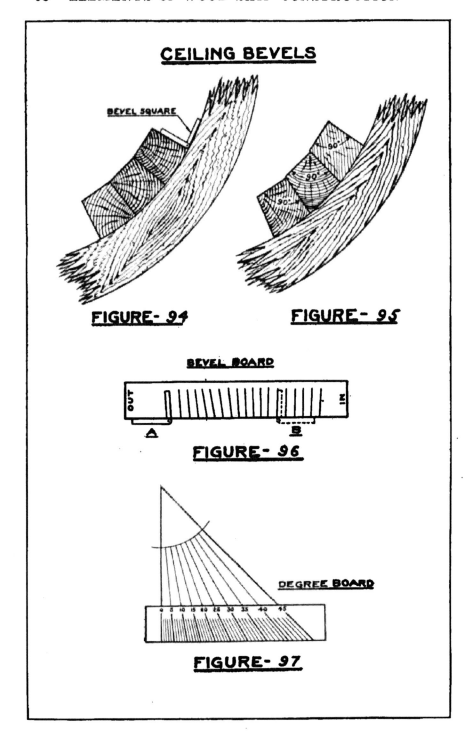

CEILING BEVELS

BEVEL SQUARE

FIGURE- 94

FIGURE- 95

BEVEL BOARD

OUT   IN

A   B

FIGURE- 96

DEGREE BOARD

FIGURE- 97

bevel board. It is not always necessary to number them. If they are taken, say at every other frame, and in order, then it is only necessary for the bevel taker to remember where he started taking the bevels.

The drawings show the beveled edges of the ceiling fitting together for their full width, but it is quite common to fit them together over only two-thirds their width. Where this is done the line for working, or sawing the timber to bevel has to be placed on the inboard face. Also in many yards the ceiling is ordered dressed only on one side, and since the dressed side is the inboard side it is much more convenient to have the cutting line on this side. But the bevel has been taken for the outboard side, and it therefore must be converted into the proper bevel reading from the inboard side. This is a very simple operation and need not be at all confusing if a little system is followed.

Mark one end of the bevel board "OUT" and the other end "IN." Then in transferring the bevels to the bevel board hold the bevel with the handle pointing as at "A." When taking the bevels off the board, for marking on the inboard face of the ceiling, hold the handle of the bevel as at "B" toward "IN." If the strake is to be marked out on the outboard face hold the bevel with the handle as at "A" or toward "OUT."

The bevels, as marked on the timber, must read in degrees, and must be marked under or standing as the case may be. The degree board is about the most convenient device for converting the angles to degrees. It is best laid out as shown in Fig. 97, and if well made will serve a multitude of uses around the ship.

The widths of the strakes are measured on the outboard faces, and when they are lined, or marked out, on the inboard faces, due allowance must be made for the amount of bevel at each point where the width of the strake is measured.

When ceiling strakes are to be fitted at the bilge or at any point where there is curvature in the frame the outboard faces must be worked off to fay to the frame. In working this face care should be used to take the same amount off each outboard corner so that the bevels will remain correct. The correct shape for working the outside face can be easily found by scribing fids, or small molds from the frames. At the ends of the ship, where the frames change shape rapidly, this should be done at frequent intervals. Experienced men will often estimate the shape with sufficient accuracy.

All ceiling is generally scarfed flat with outboard nibs feathered against the frames. It as also quite common to hold the lengths of these scarfs to two frame spaces, unless the depth of the scarf calls for a greater length when proportioned to rule. The inboard nibs should always be of standard depth.

The scarfs should be well shifted. A common rule is that scarfs in adjoining strake shall have not less than three frame bays between them, and scarfs falling on the same frame shall have not less than three strakes between them. It will be noted that this provides for a closer shift of scarfs than that given in the rules for scarfs in such members as the clamps, shelves and waterways. This is due to the fact that the lengths of ceiling timbers, being generally less than the lengths of clamp strakes, etc., do not permit as great shift of scarfs as can be obtained with the longer timbers.

Ceiling fastening, is commonly driven in the center of the frame timber as shown in Fig. 93. This arrangement reserves the space from the center to edge of the timber for the planking fastening. The staggered arrangement shown in Fig. 92 is an unusual one.

Most ceiling is square fastened, that is, four bolts to each frame are driven, two of them being button-headed bolts driven from the inside to within about one inch of the outside of the frame, and two being headed blunt bolts driven from the outside and clinched over rings on the inside. All of the fastening driven from the outside must be set into the frame to clear the dubbing.

In addition to the above fastening, each strake is

usually edge bolted, in alternate frame bays with drifts long enough to pass through two and one-half strakes. In exceptional cases these bolts are driven in each bay. The customary arrangement of these edge bolts is shown in Fig. 92. In Fig. 93 there are no edge bolts, and the bolts driven from the outside are button-headed bolts instead of headed blunt bolts. This is an unusual arrangement.

Thin bottom ceiling, not over five inches thick may be fastened with standard boat spikes. If thicker than this it should be fastened with button-headed drifts as shown in Fig. 92. All of these are of course driven from the inside. Fig. 93 shows thin ceiling between decks fastened with spikes, also thin bottom ceiling fastened in the same manner.

In closing this discussion of ceiling, it may be stated, in order that the reader may obtain a better idea of the reasons for the marked differences in the ceiling shown in Figs. 92 and 93, that the type shown in 92 is used on a vessel which is strengthened with diagonal steel straps on the outside of the frames, while the type shown in Fig. 93, is used in a vessel that is double diagonally planked in the manner indicated in Fig. 85, and which is further reinforced by a belt of steel work in way of the bulwarks.

POINTERS AND TRANSOMS

Pointers are placed in vessels for two reasons, the first being to furnish additional stiffening to the hull at the locality where the pointer is placed, to aid in resisting panting movements and stresses, and the second, to add additional strength against torsional strains such as are experienced at the ends of a ship when rolling heavily at sea.

There may be from one to three pointers at each end of the ship, depending upon the size of the ship and the designer's ideas. Fig. 98 shows a single bow pointer, and Fig. 99 two stern pointers.

Pointers are set on top of the ceiling. They should be joined together at their lower ends and should extend upward at least to the first deck. At the lower ends, a natural crook hook, or a straight grained crutch is generally fitted, thus tying the two halves of the pointer securely together. Figs. 100 and 101 show characteristic shapes and arrangements of bow and stern pointers.

Where pointers abut deadwood, as in pointer "B," Fig. 99, the crutch, or hook, is sometimes omitted. If fitted, it would in this case, be formed from a straight grained timber and would rest on top of the deadwood.

Pointers may be cut from solid timber, or they may be built up in laminated form as shown in Fig. 104. As the latter form is much the easiest to fit in place and has fully as much strength as the solid type it is coming more generally into common use.

Where the pointers are cut from the solid, molds giving the proper shape, must be lifted from the ship. The method of lifting these molds is shown in Fig. 103 and may be explained as follows:

Since the pointer does not vary in siding its seat upon the ceiling may be scribed by two parallel lines, one even with the upper face of the pointer, and the other even with the lower face, the distance between the two lines representing the sided dimension of the pointer. These two lines are indicated in the figure, as being scribed on the ceiling, but the limitations of drawing prevent showing the ceiling while still maintaining the clearness of the other essential details.

Now, at the upper end fit end cleat "A" against the ceiling and in such position that the edge and corner "C" will set square with the upper and lower faces of the pointer, or, which amounts to the same thing, square with the molds shown in the figure. Then at the lower end fit end cleat "B" so that its edge "C" is parallel to edge "C" of end cleat "A." Fit intermediate cleats sufficiently close together to hold molds in proper position for scribing. It is not necessary that these intermediate cleats be square with the molds, but their upper and lower ends should be in line with the corresponding ends of the end cleats, and each

POINTERS AND TRANSOMS

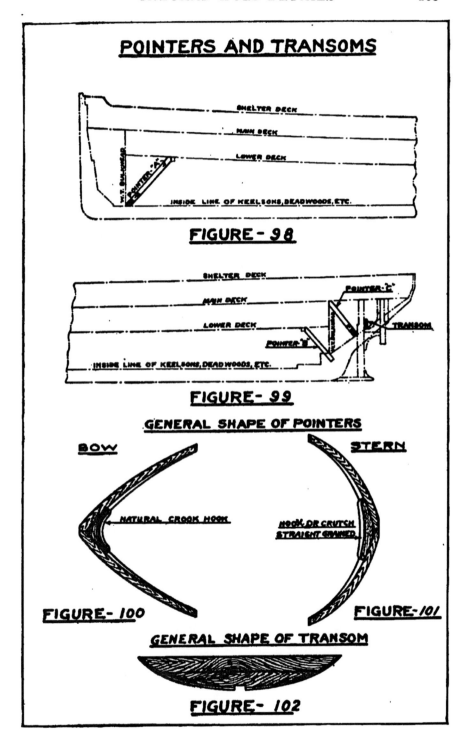

FIGURE - 98

FIGURE - 99

GENERAL SHAPE OF POINTERS

BOW

STERN

NATURAL CROOK HOOK

HOOK, OR CRUTCH STRAIGHT GRAINED

FIGURE - 100

FIGURE - 101

GENERAL SHAPE OF TRANSOM

FIGURE - 102

end should land exactly on one of the lines scribed on the ceiling. It will be seen that the length of the cleats will be the same as the sided dimension of the pointer, or the distance between the two lines, and that the upper mold will be held with its lower face even with the line, while the lower mold will be held with its upper face even with the line. Each mold should be scribed on the face that is even with the line.

The molds, which have been previously roughed out to approximate shape, are now set on the cleats and scribed and trimmed until they exactly fit the ceiling. Then with the molds tacked in the position where they fit, scribe the marks shown at edges "C" at cleats "A" and "B" on each mold. Note that there are two marks on each mold at end cleat "A," one for locating the molds longitudinally, and the other for locating the molds laterally. Hence the necessity for setting this cleat square with the molds. At end cleat "B" it is necessary to locate the molds laterally only, hence but one mark is required.

Now, by squaring a line around the timber, corresponding to the upper side of end cleat "A" and gauging another line around the timber lengthwise and corresponding to the edges "C," the workman is enabled to spot the two molds, each on the proper face of the timber and in its proper relative position to the other mold. Thus the outboard face, *i. e.*, the face fitting the ceiling may be marked out and cut. The inboard face of the pointer is scribed or gauged from the outboard face. Very often the pointer is tapered in molding, and where this is done care should be taken to keep the same molded widths at corresponding points on the upper and lower faces. This will keep the inboard face parallel with the ceiling in the vertical direction and gives a nice appearance.

Expert workmen very often fit only the upper mold, in which case the faying face of the jointer is determined by bevels, taken between the mold and the ceiling.

Hooks and crutches are scribed in the same manner as will later be explained for hanging knees.

In fitting pointers it is necessary, after the timber has been worked to proper shape, to spot bore the face that fits the ceiling, in way of all bolt heads, etc.

The operation of fitting the laminated pointers is so simple that no detailed explanation is required, except, perhaps, to remind the workman that the various timbers making up the pointer must be carefully selected for bending. Each course, or lamination, should be well steamed and sprung into place while hot. It is necessary also to fasten each course with boat spikes as it is sprung in place. These are generally driven in way of the frame bays so that the frame space will be kept clear for the through fastening, which is not driven until all of the laminations are in place.

The bolted, or through, fastening is generally the same for solid or laminated pointers and usually consists of four-headed blunt bolts at each frame, all driven from the outside and clinched over rings on the inside. These, of course, like ceiling bolts are driven before the planking is put on. Additional fastening is provided in way of the hook or crutch, this being in much the same proportion and arrangement as that described later for hanging knees.

Where the clamp arrangement is such as to permit, the upper ends of the pointers are sometimes landed against a beam, to which they are connected by a root, or natural crook, knee.

Transoms are generally located as shown in Fig. 99, though they may be fitted abaft the rudder post as well as the stern, or propeller post. They are usually built up on top of the ceiling and are located where they will best correct the deficiency of thwartship strength in way of the half frames or cants. A typical shape for the transom is shown in Fig. 102 and it will be noted that it is built up solid like a small bulkhead. Transoms are thoroughly bolted through the ceiling into the frame, a large proportion of the bolts being generally driven from the outside and clinched over rings on the inside. They should also be well bolted into the stern or rudder post, to whichever they happen to be fitted.

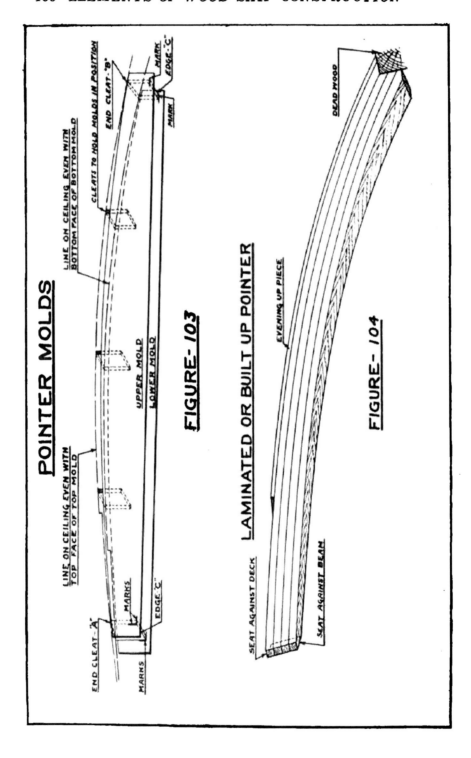

POINTER MOLDS

MARK EDGE "C"

END CLEAT "B"

MARK

CLEATS TO HOLD MOLDS IN POSITION

LINE ON CEILING EVEN WITH BOTTOM FACE OF BOTTOM MOLD

UPPER MOLD

LOWER MOLD

LINE ON CEILING EVEN WITH TOP FACE OF TOP MOLD

END CLEAT "A"

MARKS

MARKS

EDGE "C"

FIGURE - 103

LAMINATED OR BUILT UP POINTER

DEAD WOOD

EVENING UP PIECE

SEAT AGAINST DECK

SEAT AGAINST BEAM

FIGURE - 104

HOLD BULKHEADS

Hold bulkheads in wood ships are fitted for two general purposes. The first is, to subdivide the interior of the hull into small compartments so that if any one of the compartments is flooded, through damage to the hull, etc., the ship will still remain afloat. The second purpose is to provide additional thwartship stiffening against what is known as keel hogging and also against torsional strains.

Two types of hold bulkheads are in use, that shown in Fig. 105 being known as the "diagonal" hold bulkhead and that shown in Fig. 106 as the "solid log" bulkhead. The figures are practically self-explanatory and will require very little discussion.

It will be noted in Fig. 105 that the diagonal bulkhead planking in the lower hold is placed between two stanchions, which are opposite each other, these stanchions being heavily bolted together. Between decks, in the same bulkhead, stanchions are shown on but one side of the planking, the lighter construction here being due to the fact that the water pressure, should the hold become flooded, would be much less at the top than at the bottom of the bulkhead. If there were no decking laid on the lower tier of beams to stiffen the bulkhead at this point, then it would be necessary to extend the stanchions on both sides to the deck above.

To insure watertightness two thicknesses of tarred felt are laid between the courses of diagonal planking, care being taken to properly break joints. The border coamings are calked in the usual manner.

In general, the fastening will be as shown in the figure. The diagonal planking fastening, which is not shown, consists of standard boat spikes. Each plank should be well spiked not only at the ends but to each stanchion on one side. Obviously it would be impossible to spike this planking to stanchions on both sides.

These bulkheads are generally faced toward the expected

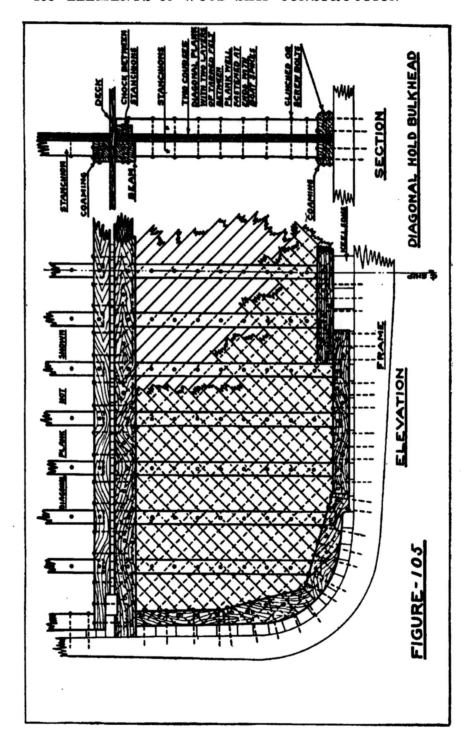

FIGURE-105

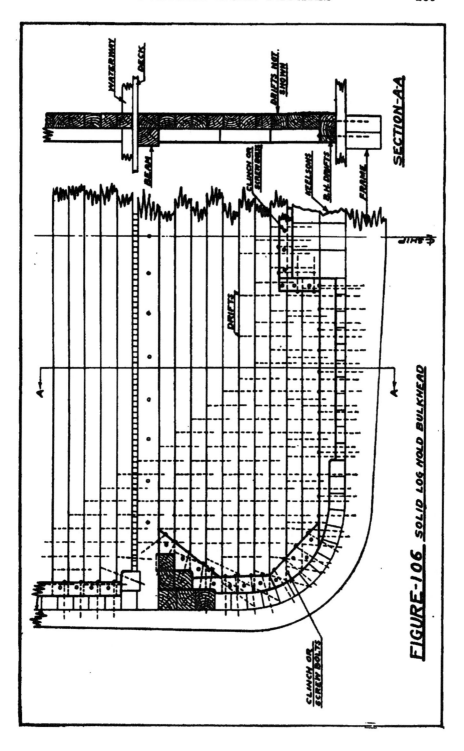

FIGURE-106 SOLID LOG HOLD BULKHEAD

source of water pressure, hence, bulkheads forward of midship would be faced forward and those aft of that point would be faced aft. The term "face" as here used is taken to mean the side of the bulkhead opposite the deck beam against which it is built. The bulkhead in Fig. 105 would under this rule face to the reader's right, and it will be noticed that the single stanchions between decks are on the back side.

Solid log bulkheads, such as that shown in Fig. 106 may be put down without the extra heavy border timbers, or coamings, which have been shown in the figure, though it may be considered the best practice to use these heavy coamings as they afford room for additional fastening around the border which is often quite essential. It will be noted that at the side of the ship the bulkhead timbers are not landed on top of the coaming timbers as at the bottom, but are continued past them to and against the ceiling.

The arrangement of edge drift bolts in the bulkhead timbers as shown here is typical. Each bolt passes through two and one-half strakes. Those bolts at and near the bottom of the bulkhead should be close spaced as shown in the figure, the reason for this being much the same as that for adding the extra set of stanchions to the diagonal bulkhead in the lower hold.

These bulkheads must be calked all over and for this purpose calking seams must be run on all timbers. These seams should be small, that is not over one and one-half inches deep with a total opening of about three-sixteenths of one inch.

The ceiling, in way of all bulkheads, whether diagonal, or solid log construction, must be made water tight either by wedging or calking. Calking and paying heavily with pitch seems to be the most highly approved procedure.

DECK BEAMS

Deck beams for weather decks must always have a round up, or to use another term, camber. The standard amount

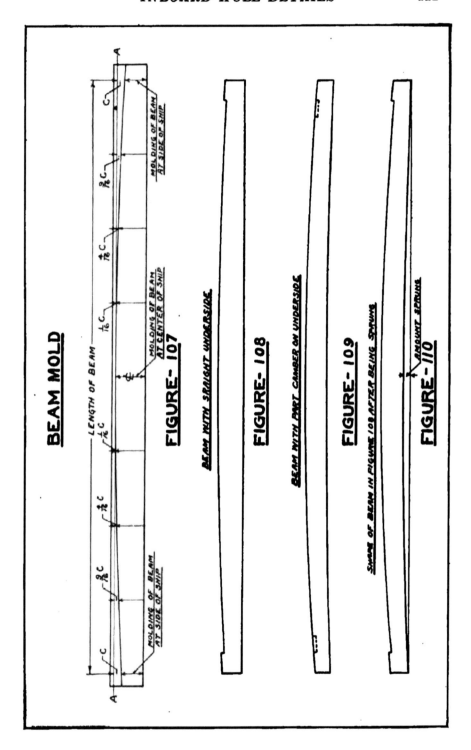

BEAM MOLD

FIGURE- 107

FIGURE- 108

FIGURE- 109

FIGURE- 110

of this camber, or spring from a straight line, is one-quarter of one inch for each foot of length of the beam. In wood ships, however, the amount of camber is very often reduced to about three-fourths of the standard camber.

Only a part of the camber is cut on the beam. The balance of the required amount is obtained by springing the center of the beam upward after the ends have been fastened down in the ship. This operation, while performed with heavy jacks, is generally called "pumping the beams."

The relative amounts of camber to be sawn and sprung into the beam depend largely upon the difference between the molding of the beam at the center and that at the ends, and the length of the beam.

Beams of ordinary proportions may generally be sprung about one-eighth of one inch for each foot of length although this must be regarded as very near the limit, and it is often best to hold the spring to about a tenth of one inch per foot of length. Thus a beam forty feet in length may be sprung from four to five inches. The balance of whatever camber may be required will have to be cut in the beam.

As an example let us suppose that we have a beam forty feet in length as above and that the required camber is eight inches, and that of this amount it is considered safe to spring five inches. This leaves three inches of camber to be cut in the beam. Now, if the required molding at the center is fourteen inches, and at the ends, eleven inches, the difference between the two moldings is three inches and we may cut the camber on this beam on one side only, thus leaving the underside straight as shown in Fig. 108. (The molding in this type of beam at the end is measured at the bottom of the hook. In the type shown in Fig. 109 it is measured at the end of the beam.)

Again, let us suppose, that with the same length of beam and required camber, the required molding at the center is fourteen inches and at the ends thirteen inches. Now, the amount of camber to be cut in the beam is three inches and the difference between the moldings is but one inch, therefore it will be seen with a little study that we must cut two inches of camber on the under side of this beam, in order to be able to cut three inches on the top and still maintain the required moldings. We will then have a beam of the type shown in Fig. 109.

After it has been determined what camber to cut in the beam, a beam mold is made for the midship beam, having this amount of camber. This may be easily laid out by what is known as the "one, four, nine rule," as shown in Fig. 107. This is the same rule that has been previously given for the laying out of spring points on the keel and need not be further explained here.

This same mold is then used for scribing the tops of all beams except those near the after end of the ship, where the beams must be flattened out in order to fair the centerline of the deck into the knuckle or rim. If the beams are of the type shown in Fig. 109 then the mold may be made with both edges cambered as required, so that the beam may be scribed from the one mold.

The amount that the beams must flatten out at the stern to avoid a hump in the deck depends upon the shape of the deck at that point and the amount of sheer. Very often the deck line inside the frames is dropped slightly just forward of the stern so that the beams will not have to be flattened so much. No rule can be given for this operation and experience is about the only teacher that will enable the workman to obtain uniformly good results. However it may be stated that in many cases, all of the beams may be molded and cut to the same camber, the flattening out at the stern being gauged by pumping the beams to a stiff fairing batten set in the centerline.

HANGING KNEES

Where heavy shelves are not fitted, it is the rule to place a hanging knee under each end of each beam. This practice is confined principally to the Western Coast where there is a great supply of natural crook fir knees available.

8

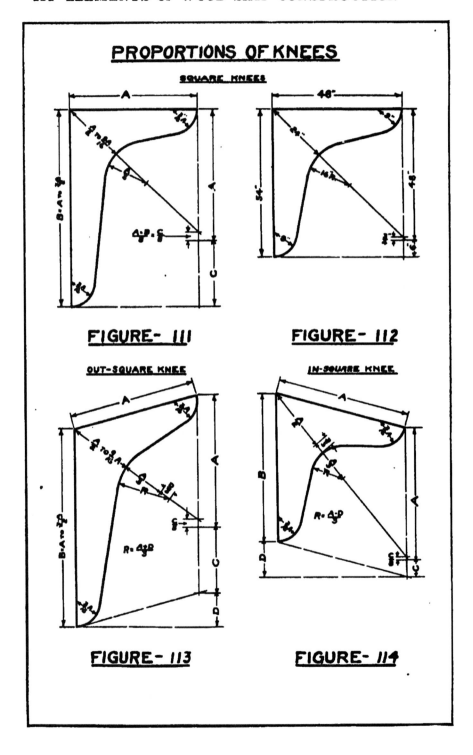

FIGURE- 111

FIGURE- 112

FIGURE- 113

FIGURE- 114

They are cut from the roots of fir trees and are remarkably strong.

Heretofore there have been no rules for proportioning these knees beyond the rough rules devised by the ship carpenters in the yards. The author has, therefore, after giving the subject some study, devised the proportioning rules shown in Figs. 111 to 114 inclusive. These rules should of course be used with some discretion, but for the great majority of knees of the ordinary proportions they will produce strong knees having a pleasing appearance.

The short leg of the knee is generally called "the root" and the long leg "the trunk" as this is the position in which the knee is cut from the stump of the tree.

There is no very definite relation between the thickness of knees and the length of root and trunk. The following table gives the range of proportions most generally used.

Thickness	Length of Root "A"
12 inches	48 to 60 inches
10 inches	40 to 48 inches
8 inches	36 to 45 inches
6 inches	24 to 36 inches
4 inches	16 to 24 inches

Typical knee fastenings and the method of scribing them in are shown in Figs. 115 to 117 inclusive. In Fig. 115 some of the bolts are driven from the inside while the balance are button-headed bolts driven from the outside and clinched inside. In Fig. 116 all of the bolts where possible except the throat bolt are driven from the outside and clinched inside.

The scribing and fitting of a knee is in reality a very simple operation, the principal part of which is shown in Fig. 117. The knee is first roughed out so that when shored up against the beam and ceiling it will stand close enough everywhere to permit scribing, or more properly speaking, pricking. Then with dividers held in the positions indicated in the figure prick points are made at frequent in-

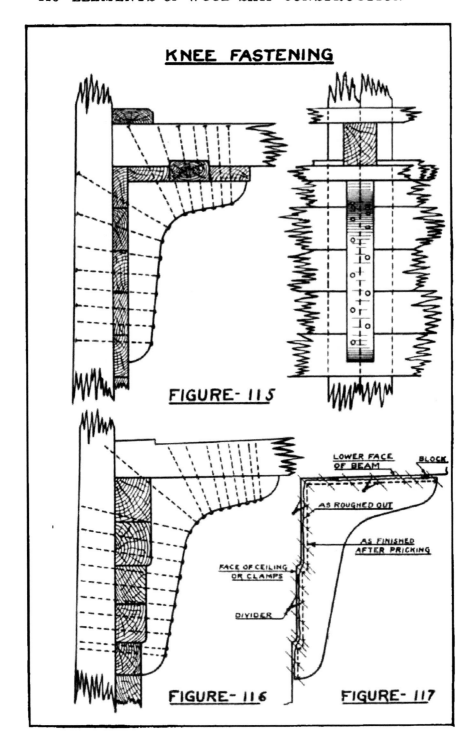

KNEE FASTENING

FIGURE-115

FIGURE-116

FIGURE-117

LOWER FACE OF BEAM

BLOCK

AS ROUGHED OUT

AS FINISHED AFTER PRICKING

FACE OF CEILING OR CLAMPS

DIVIDER

tervals on both sides of the knee, which when joined with a line give the cutting limit for a fit. In the figure short lines have been drawn to indicate the relative position of the two points of the divider. Care must be taken to hold the divider at the same angle at all points. If this is done the knee can be pricked and cut in at one operation no matter what the shape of the ceiling, or clamps. Care must also be taken to so adjust the knee for pricking that the proper amount of material will still remain in the knee after it has been cut to the prick points.

Ceiling and clamp fastenings should be kept clear of knees, but where they happen to land in the way, the faying face of the knee must be spot bored to clear them.

All hanging knees set square with the centerline of the ship, but the inboard face of the knee should be so dressed off that it will parallel the ceiling in the fore and aft direction. This is done by first determining the amount of bevel the hanging leg of the knee is to have and sawing a corresponding bevel on the inner face. This is not done for the purpose of securing strength, but mainly to give a pleasing and workmanlike appearance to the knee after it has been placed in the ship.

HOLD STANCHIONS

Stanchions, or pillars, must be fitted under the beams for supporting the deck above and the cargo load that may be placed on that deck. The greater the number of decks above a stanchion or pillar the heavier it must be, and the more securely should it be fastened. There are many ways of fitting and fastening hold stanchions some of which are shown in Figs. 118 to 121 inclusive.

Hold stanchions as a rule are arranged on the centerline of the ship, one under each beam. Where the deck load is not very heavy stanchions may be set under alternate beams, there being a stringer to support the beams under which there are no stanchions, as shown in Fig. 119.

When stanchions are set off the centerline and wide spaced they are called pillars. When set at the corners of

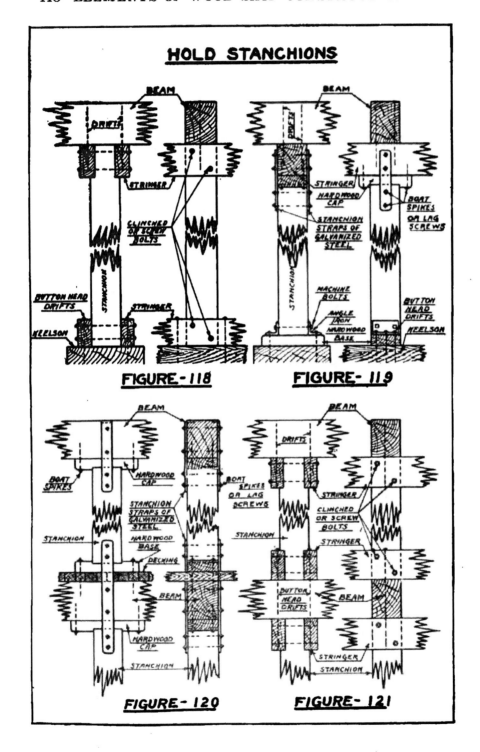

HOLD STANCHIONS

FIGURE - 118

FIGURE - 119

FIGURE - 120

FIGURE - 121

hatches they become quarter pillars. If set out in the hold and away from the hatch they are more often referred to as hold pillars. As before stated there are many different combinations and arrangements used, as each different type of ship presents a problem in itself, and the stanchions therein must be arranged to carry the particular loads existing in the vessel.

By far the most important detail of stanchion and pillar fitting is the end fastening. In any type used care must be taken to so arrange the irons and bolts at the ends of the stanchion in such manner as to secure the greatest strength. Figures 118 and 119 show two arrangements where there is but one deck. Figures 120 and 121 show two arrangements where the stanchioning must pass through an intermediate deck. These arrangements would also hold good where the stanchions pass through a line of hold beams, the only difference being that the decking would be left out. This has been done in Fig. 121.

In some localities on smaller vessels the stanchion straps are fastened with boat spikes, but this cannot be considered good practice for large vessels.

GLOSSARY

Hoods—The first and last members in a strake of ceiling, planking, etc. The forehood abuts the stem or apron. The afterhood abuts the sternpost, rim, or after deadwood. The term *hood end* refers to the forward end of the forehood or the after end of the afterhood according as it may be designated, *forward hood end*, or *after hood end*.

Keel Hogging—A term used to describe the condition when the keel hogs as the rest of the ship remains in apparently good alignment. The condition is caused by weak floors.

Luff—As in the expression *luff of the bow* which is used to describe an indefinite point about midway between the stem and the parallel body where the curvature and flare are very pronounced. Also used to describe certain arrangement of tackle more commonly known as a *watch tackle*.

Peak—The space between the last hold bulkheads and the ends of the ship. This space at the bow is known as the fore peak. At the stern it is called the after peak.

Panting—A term used to describe the breathing movement that takes place in a ship's hull caused by pitching in a heavy sea. Panting may be very pronounced at certain localities at the ends of the vessel, particularly at the bow just abaft the collision bulkhead. Very often extra beams called panting beams are fitted in this vicinity to counteract this movement, which is very destructive to the hull. Pointers are also used to overcome panting strains.

Pay—To fill a seam as with cement or pitch, or to paint a seam with paint or oil. Paying is the act of filling the seam, etc.

Room—Space in which anything is to be fitted.

Spile—To determine the shape of a plank necessary to fit a certain line on the hull. For this purpose the workman uses a spiling batten, this being a thin flexible board which is bent to the frames or hull at the point where it is desired to take a spiling. By transferring points from the desired line to the spiling batten, the necessary shape of the plank to fit the line is determined.

Snipe—To cut off the end of a timber on an angle so that it runs to a point, or nearly to a point.

Strake—A course of planking, ceiling, or any other member of the hull continuing fore and aft unbroken except by butts or scarfs.

FOREWORD TO CHAPTER IV

The author desires at this time to again remind the reader that the details of wood ship construction which may be considered the best practice in the different localities where such ships are built are so much at variance in scantlings, arrangement and fastening that it is impossible to show and describe all of them within the limits of these chapters. Practice that is considered good in one locality may not be so considered in another. Types of ships favored in the different localities are different. Individual experiences and opinions differ according to the measure of success operators have had with certain types. The sizes and character of timbers available for the construction of wood ships in different localities vary greatly, and have a very decided influence on design. Taking it all in all, modern designs of wood ships show the tendency of designers in different sections not only to approach the problem from widely divergent angles of experience and observation, but very often upon absolutely different basic principles.

However, even with the confusing mass of contradictory ideas the recent wood shipbuilding has produced, there is a certain relation between the parts of a ship which may be said to exist regardless of their detail scantling arrangements. It is therefore felt that if the reader is enabled to familiarize himself with one or two types of construction in detail, he will at once recognize similar parts of other ships though they may differ in their arrangement.

In the last chapter the tabulation of the order of procedure ended with the fitting of the lower hold bulkheads and pointers. Since this chapter deals with deck details, the work outlined herein would properly begin with the setting of the deck beams. As soon as the beams have been fastened at the ends and pumped to the proper camber, the hatch framing must be gotten out and fitted in place. Breast hooks, deck hooks, chocks for receiving the fastening at the ends of the decking, and mast partners are also fitted at this time. It may also be found convenient to fit at this time such heavy chocking as may be required in way of deck fittings, winches, etc. All hatch coamings except those to be placed on top of the decking should be fitted and fastened before the decking is laid. Light chocking in way of vents, pipes, etc., is not fitted until the pipes are in place.

The exercise of a reasonable amount of care in seeing that all of the above details are in place before the decking is laid will often save much trouble and expense later on.

Hatch details, such as covers, strongbacks, etc., are gotten out at any time when the arrangement of the work permits.

Tabulation of the Order of Procedure—Deck Details

MAIN OPERATION	COINCIDENT OPERATION
Setting of deck beams.	Pumping and shoring beams to camber.
Fitting of fore and afters, half beams, lodging knees, etc., at hatches.	Setting stanchions; fitting mast partners, breast hooks, deck hooks, chocks, hatch coamings, etc.
Laying of waterways.	Fitting of shelves or hanging knees.
Laying of the decking.	
Completion of hold bulkheads.	

The above tabulation refers to the deck only. While this work is going on, and as soon as the ceiling fastening has been completed, the outside planking is started, and in most cases the planking and the work on the deck will be going on at the same time.

CHAPTER IV

DECK DETAILS

DECK BEAMS, HALF BEAMS, ETC.

In the last chapter the method of obtaining the camber on the beams was explained, and it will be remembered that only a part of the camber is ordinarily cut on the beam, the balance being obtained by springing. In the case of half beams and short beams at the ends of the vessel the full camber must be cut as there is no opportunity of springing such beams. For this purpose molds are made, having the correct full camber for both the upper and lower faces of the half beams, or short beams as the case may be. The beams are then laid out by these molds and worked to the full camber.

The correct shape for half-beam molds is obtained by laying out a full camber curve for the full beam of the ship as has been previously explained, and fitting the mold to that portion of the curve over which the half beam actually extends. One mold is generally sufficient for all half beams. This method applies to all half beams in any type of hatch framing.

Beams and half beams are generally fastened at the outer ends with two drift bolts driven well into the clamps. For the beams, this is largely a temporary fastening to hold them in place while they are being sprung to the full camber, after which the knees or shelves are fitted and the main beam fastening driven. Very often, in order to assist the drift bolts in holding down the ends of the beams during the pumping it is necessary to clamp heavy blocks just above the beams and on the inside of the frames or stanchions in such position that wedges may be driven between the lower ends of the blocks and the ends of the beams. This keeps the fastening from starting and in a little while after the beams have been sprung they may be removed. Half beams are not fitted until the beams have been sprung to their full camber and the hatch trimmers have been placed. The outer ends of half beams receive the same fastening as described for beam ends.

The hold stanchions may or may not be fitted immediately after the beams are sprung. Very often it is more convenient to fit temporary shores to hold the beams up until such time as the hold stanchions can be fitted. Where shores are used there should be two to each beam, one on each side of the center-line, or location of the hold stanchion, so as to leave the stanchion location clear.

All beams should be worked and finished smooth before being placed in the ship. The lower corners are commonly chamfered except in way of shelves or hanging knees. If the deck frame is properly handled there should be practically no dubbing necessary to secure a fair surface for laying the decking.

It will be noticed that the beam spacing in Fig. 122 is the same as that of the frames, while in Figs. 123 and 124 it is different. Where hanging knees are used in place of shelves the tendency is to make the beam spacing the same as that of the frames with a beam against each frame, as then all of the knee fastenings will land in the frames. Where the beam spacing is not the same as that of the frames as in Fig. 124 chocks to receive fastening are fitted in the frame bays in way of hanging knees not landing on the frames. In Fig. 123 where shelves are used there is no particular disadvantage in having a beam space different from the frame space, but even in this construction the modern tendency is to make the two spacings practically the same.

HATCH FRAMING ·

Three types of hatch framing have been selected as being the most representative of the many different constructions used.

That shown in Fig. 122, type I, is in use at the present

time in large vessels having either no shelf strakes or very
light shelf strakes, in either case the beams being fitted
with hanging knees. The figure is shown without shelf
and with hanging knees spotted under each beam.

It will be noted that the fore and after, or hatch trimmer
as it happens to be called on these vessels, is dapped into
the hatch beams and connected thereto at each end with
a large lodging knee. The half beams are in turn dapped
into the hatch trimmer and are connected thereto with
flat iron straps turned down over the inside of the trimmer
and well fastened with countersunk head bolts into the
half beam. These daps should be cut with a standing
bevel from the top of the hatch beam, or fore and after
(hatch trimmer), and in addition should have a step or landing
worked about halfway down the side of the beam or fore
and after, as shown in the figures. The bevel should be
such as to carry the dap in on the upper face not to exceed
2 to $2\frac{1}{2}$ inches, according to the size of the beam, and the
step may be made from $\frac{1}{2}$ to $\frac{3}{4}$ inch wide. Not only does
this form of dap make the fitting and fastening of
the trimmers and half beams easier, but it actually adds
to the strength of the connection.

Where fore and afters, or trimmers, are deeper in molding
than the hatch beams, they are generally dapped up from
below as shown in section C-C, Fig. 122, and the dap is
made without bevel. These rules in general apply to all
hatch framing.

The various sections below the main figure show the
shape of the end and side coamings both for the weather
and lower decks. Note that the end coaming is set on the
beam and that it can therefore be placed and fastened when
the side coamings are fitted. The absence of individual
lodging knees at the ends of the hatch and half beams
in these vessels is compensated for by fitting diagonal
steel straps on the beams before the decking is laid, these
straps being set in flush with the tops of the beams and
extending from side to side of the ship. At their ends they
are riveted to a steel deck stringer plate which in these

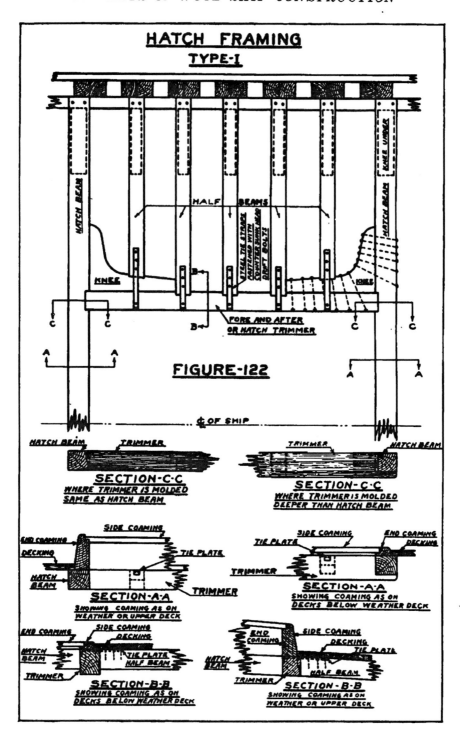

HATCH FRAMING
TYPE-I

FIGURE-122

SECTION-C-C
WHERE TRIMMER IS MOLDED
SAME AS HATCH BEAM

SECTION-C-C
WHERE TRIMMER IS MOLDED
DEEPER THAN HATCH BEAM

SECTION-A-A
SHOWING COAMING AS ON
WEATHER OR UPPER DECK

SECTION-A-A
SHOWING COAMING AS ON
DECKS BELOW WEATHER DECK

SECTION-B-B
SHOWING COAMING AS ON
DECKS BELOW WEATHER DECK

SECTION-B-B
SHOWING COAMING AS ON
WEATHER OR UPPER DECK

vessels takes the place of the waterways. A section showing one form of this stringer plate is shown in Fig. 131.

Type II, Fig. 123, also shows a construction that is now in use in large ships. Here there are heavy shelf strakes under the beam ends in place of hanging knees. The fore and after is dapped into the hatch beams and connected thereto by a small lodging knee, while the half beams are connected to the fore and after in the same manner. Typical arrangements of fastening for these lodging knees are shown.

Another feature of this construction is the continuous stringer, on each side, under the fore and afters, which extends fore and aft at least to the peak bulkheads. This is fitted not only to furnish additional strength in way of the hatches, which is quite essential, but to add to the strength of the ship itself.

Coamings in this type of hatch are generally fitted in the same manner as those shown in Fig. 122.

Type III, Fig. 124, is a construction that is much used where the beams are fitted with hanging knees to the exclusion of all shelves. Here the fore and after is fitted in the usual manner and the half beams have lodging knees at each end. Chocks are shown fitted between the beam ends over the clamps.

These beam chocks are in reality a part of the beam fastening and they are quite commonly fitted to all beams in the ship and not only to those in way of the hatches as the reader might be led to believe through the fact that owing to the limits of the page they are here shown only in way of the hatch framing. Further on in this chapter are details showing these chocks without respect to the hatch framing. Beam chocks are not fitted in ships using the style of hatch framing shown in Fig. 122. They may or may not be used with the type of construction shown in Fig. 123, and are invariably used with the construction shown in Fig. 124.

In way of lodging knees they are extra fastened as shown in the figure. In any event they receive from two to four drift bolts into the clamps, and also have a hardwood

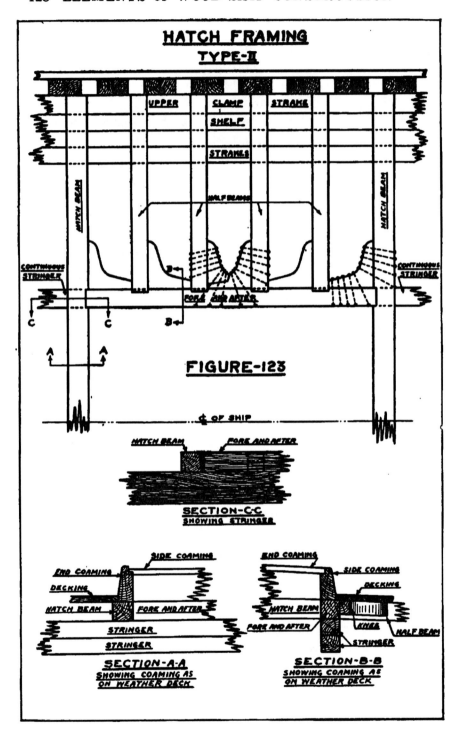

HATCH FRAMING
TYPE-II

FIGURE-123

SECTION-C-C
SHOWING STRINGER

SECTION-A-A
SHOWING COAMING AS
ON WEATHER DECK

SECTION-B-B
SHOWING COAMING AS
ON WEATHER DECK

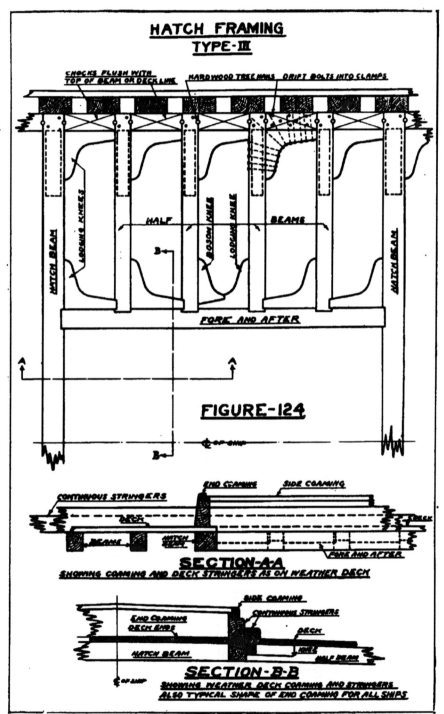

HATCH FRAMING
TYPE-III

CHOCKS FLUSH WITH TOP OF BEAM OR DECK LINE   HARDWOOD TREE NAILS   DRIFT BOLTS INTO CLAMPS

HATCH BEAM   LODGING KNEES   HALF   BOSOM KNEE   LODGING KNEE   BEAMS   HATCH BEAM

B

FORE AND AFTER

A   A

FIGURE-124

B   ℄ OF SHIP

CONTINUOUS STRINGERS   END COAMING   SIDE COAMING

DECK   DECK

BEAMS   HATCH BEAM   FORE AND AFTER

SECTION-A-A
SHOWING COAMING AND DECK STRINGERS AS ON WEATHER DECK

SIDE COAMING

END COAMING   CONTINUOUS STRINGERS
DECK ENDS   DECK

HATCH BEAM   KNEE   HALF BEAM

SECTION-B-B
SHOWING WEATHER DECK COAMING AND STRINGERS
ALSO TYPICAL SHAPE OF END COAMING FOR ALL SHIPS

℄ OF SHIP

treenail set in the joint between beam and chock at each end to assist in locking the beam in place. In some cases the chocks are omitted in way of the lodging knees, the latter then being fitted direct to the frame. Where this is done and the beam spacing is the same as that of the frames with a beam against each frame, the bays must be chocked to provide room for driving sufficient knee fastening.

Continuous stringers are fitted on each side of these hatches on top of the beams and extend fore and aft at least as far as the poop and forecastle bulkheads. The side coamings are quite small and set on top of the larger of the two stringer members. The hatch end coamings set on top of the decking, and are therefore not fitted until after the decking is laid. It will be noted that the decking projects inside of the end coamings, forming a ledge which is later used as a support for the strongbacks.

HATCH COAMINGS

Three of the principal types of coamings used on weather deck hatches are shown in Figs. 125 to 127 inclusive.

Type 1, Fig. 125 may be said to be the most commonly used and is the type shown in the detail sections in Figs. 122 and 123. Both end and side coamings set on the beam and the decking is stopped against them. The corners are halved, the bottom of the timbers being left square and the top rounded to a radius. In the corner the rabbet is not turned square, but is cut across at an angle at about 45 degrees.

Figure 126 is a large corner detail of the type of coaming shown in detail sections in Fig. 124.

Here, the side coaming consists of a small timber set on top of the principal stringer member. The end coaming is worked from a solid timber. It may or may not set on top of the decking and is dapped into the continuous stringer. The dap shown in the figure is square, but very often it is cut on a bevel as shown in Fig. 127. Here the

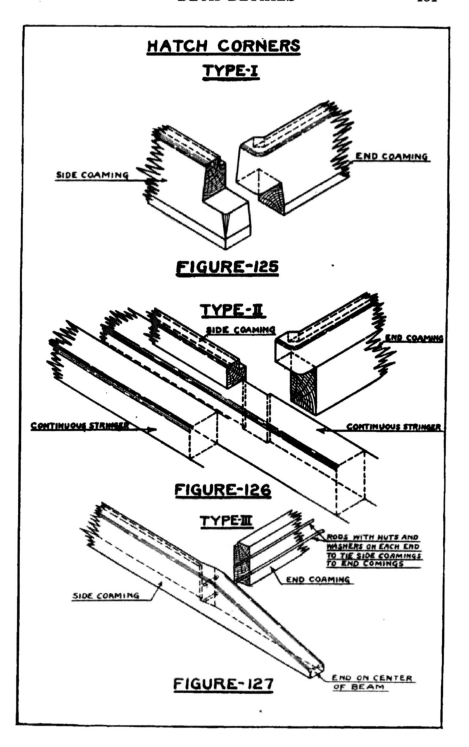

HATCH CORNERS
TYPE-I

SIDE COAMING

END COAMING

FIGURE-125

TYPE-II

SIDE COAMING

END COAMING

CONTINUOUS STRINGER

CONTINUOUS STRINGER

FIGURE-126

TYPE-III

RODS WITH NUTS AND WASHERS ON EACH END TO TIE SIDE COAMINGS TO END COMINGS

END COAMING

SIDE COAMING

END ON CENTER OF BEAM

FIGURE-127

rabbet is also cut across the corner at an angle of 45 degrees. Note that this coaming is not beveled off on the outer face below the top of the continuous stringer as this would make it very difficult to fit in the dap.

In type III Fig. 127 the side coaming is worked from a solid timber but is extended past the end coaming to the middle of about the second beam from the hatch beam. The end coaming may or may not be set on top of the decking. It is bevel dapped into the side coaming and rods with nuts on each end are fitted to hold the coamings together at the corners. Large washers are fitted under these nuts. The rabbet is turned square in the corner.

In general, side coamings are set with their inside faces plumb, and the bottom edges must therefore be beveled off where the deck carries a camber. End coamings are set with their inside faces square with the run of the deck. Where the deck carries a camber they must be scribed down to shape. Where the corners are as in Fig. 125 this may be done before the corner cuts are made. In Figs. 126 and 127, since the side coamings are generally the first to be fitted, the end coamings are scribed down after the end cuts are made and extreme care must be taken to scribe off the exact amount to get a proper fit at the ends.

Weather deck hatch coamings may vary in height from 24 to 32 inches, measured from the top of the decking to the top of the coaming, depending upon the class of the vessel and the requirements of the classification society rules under which the vessel is being built. Lower deck hatch coamings are usually made only of sufficient height to receive a proper rabbet for the covers.

Coamings are always rabbeted to receive the hatch covers. While the distance that the rabbet is cut in on the coaming may vary from about 2½ to 3½ inches its depth must always be exactly the same as the thickness of the covers, which is generally about 3½ inches.

The tops of side coamings on all decks are always made parallel with the deck. Tops of end coamings on weather decks are worked with a pitch rising toward the centerline of the ship as shown in Fig. 124, Section B-B. There is no rule for the amount of pitch to be used but it should not as a rule be less than about ½ inch to the foot. Tops of end coamings of hatches on the lower decks are made without pitch where the deck has no camber.

It is very essential that coamings be securely fastened. Generally they are fastened with large button-headed bolts, close spaced and driven from the top through coaming and beam or fore and after. Below, these bolts are either clinched over rings or fitted with nuts set up on plate washers. The heads on top of the coamings are set in counterbores which are plugged with white pine plugs set in white lead.

HATCH REINFORCING

It is impossible to set the ordinary type of hold stanchions in way of the hatches and some means must be provided for supporting, or reinforcing the deck and hatch framing in this vicinity so that it will safely carry the loads of cargo placed at these points.

In hatches where stringers are provided as in Figs. 123 and 124 it is customary to set quarter pillars at each of the four corners of the hatch, these being placed under the stringers. In hatches where the stringers are under the beams as in Fig. 124 the quarter pillars may be set three or four feet fore and aft of the ends of the hatches, provided, of course that the stringers are made strong enough to carry the additional load due to the longer span. In hatches of the type shown in Fig. 124 the quarter pillars are set directly at the hatch corners. This is also true with the design of hatch framing shown in Fig. 122. Quarter pillars are fitted and fastened in much the same manner as hold stanchions. Additional pillars may also be set under the stringers between the hatches, depending upon the distance from one hatch to the other.

In the type of hatch framing shown in Fig. 122, where there is a total absence of stringers, intermediate pillars must be set at the middle of the trimmer beams as these beams are not strong enough to carry the full cargo load. These pillars are usually made removable so that they can be taken out of the way when loading or unloading cargo.

DECK AND BREAST HOOKS

There is some confusion in different localities in the use of the terms "Breast Hook" and "Deck Hook." The author has always considered the breast hook as being properly a member landing in way of the upper clamp strake and against the apron, to both of which it is fayed. It usually is worked from a large natural crook knee. The deck hook, he has always considered as being a series of short beams, set against the apron and each other and on top of the clamps. The breast hook ties the upper clamp together and to the stem structure. The deck hook furnishes the connection between the decking, clamps and stem structure. Where the breast hook is omitted the deck hook serves both purposes. Breast hooks may be fitted where no decking is laid. Deck hooks are never fitted except where decking extends to and against the stem structure.

Figure 128 shows both of the above features of construction. It is assumed in this figure that the lower or tween decks, if any is laid, ends against the peak, or collision, bulkhead and therefore does not extend to the stem. A breast hook is shown fitted to the upper clamp strake under this line of beams.

Upper, weather, or main deck decking, is always extended to and against the apron or waterway hook, hence there would be a deck hook as shown in the figure. As before mentioned the breast hook below the deck is often omitted.

Breasthooks are fitted and fastened in much the same manner as hanging knees. Most of the bolts should be headed, driven from the outside and clinched over rings on the inside. Heavy throat bolts are driven, either headed or through rings, well into the apron and stem.

Deck hooks are generally fastened as shown in the figure. The bolts extending fore and aft should be as long as pos-

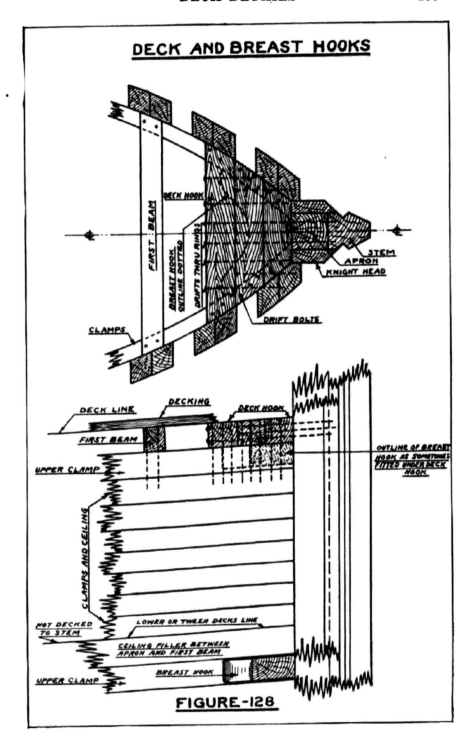

FIGURE-128

sible. Where care is exercised the timbers forming the hook may be worked to the deck camber before being placed but it is generally best to leave them a little high so that they may be dubbed to the correct camber after being fastened down. To allow for necessary dubbing the bolts fastening the deck hook to the clamps are often plain drifts set in. Where they are button-headed bolts, or plain-headed bolts driven through rings, they should be counterbored and set in.

MAST PARTNERS AND CHOCKS

Typical mast partners are shown in Fig. 129. They are not fitted until the beams have been sprung to the full camber. One of the best methods of obtaining the correct shape of the upper and lower faces of the partners so that they will fit the camber of the beams is to scribe the partner mold direct from the beams after they have been sprung.

Masts are not set square with the keel, but generally rake aft from $\frac{1}{4}$ inch to $\frac{3}{8}$ inch to the foot of height. It is necessary therefore before the partners are in place to set a line on the centerlines of the mast and ship, extending from the location of the mast step on top of the keelsons, past all of the decks and having the desired rake with the keel. If the tops of the keelsons are parallel with the keel the rake may be measured from the keelsons. An ordinary carpenter's chalk line may be used for this purpose and care must be taken to see that it is set in exactly the position that would be occupied by the center of the mast.

By measuring the distances from this line to the beams, at both the upper and lower faces, the proper location and bevel of the mast hole is obtained. This will not necessarily center on the joint between the partners.

The preliminary hole cut in the partners is usually much smaller than that finally required for the mast. If sufficient care is taken in locating the centers, the holes may be cut to within about one inch of the final diameter, and this may be done either before or after the partners have been fastened in place. The final diameter will be that of the mast plus the room required for the wedges.

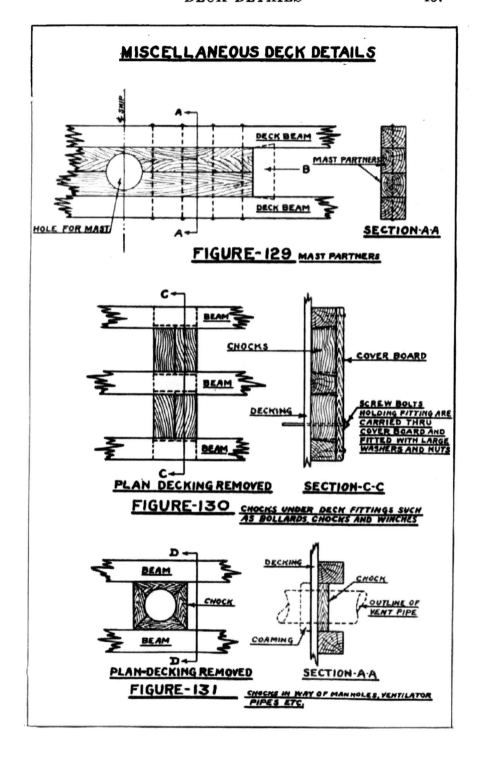

MISCELLANEOUS DECK DETAILS

FIGURE-129 MAST PARTNERS

FIGURE-130 CHOCKS UNDER DECK FITTINGS SUCH AS BOLLARDS, CHOCKS AND WINCHES

FIGURE-131 CHOCKS IN WAY OF MANHOLES, VENTILATOR PIPES ETC.

The bolts fastening the partners should pass through beam and beam and be clinched over rings on each end. Sometimes an end chock, dapped into the beams, is fitted as shown by the dotted outline at "B," but this is rather unusual in steamers.

Chocks between the beams must be placed under all deck fittings which require through fastening. They are generally dapped into the beams from below as shown in Fig. 130 and may be placed either before or after the decking is laid. If their proper locations can be determined in time it is more convenient to set them before the decking is laid.

Beneath these chocks heavy coverboards should be fitted as shown in the figure. These give a better appearance to the job and at the same time provide a necessary tie between the beams and chocks. The fastening for the coverboard and chocks usually consists of standard boat spikes and they must be kept clear of the holding down bolts for the fittings, which are to be put through later.

Chocks between beams must also be placed at the ends of the ship where decking ends land between beams as shown in Figs. 139 and 140. These chocks are not generally dapped into the beams. They should, however, be well fastened with either small-headed drifts or boat spikes.

Light chocks are also fitted where vent pipes or similar fixtures pass through the deck. These are not generally fitted until after the vent pipes are in place which is, of course also some time after the decking has been laid. A very convenient way of cutting them is shown in Fig. 131. When cut in this manner it is possible to secure a neat fit to the pipe and no other finish is required. It will be seen that with a small coaming on top of the decking, and this chock below, both fitting the pipe, it is not necessary for the hole in the decking to be cut with great accuracy. As a matter of fact, since such pipes vary slightly in size throughout their lengths, and also have overlapping joints, it would be impossible to secure a neat fit in the decking proper and still make the hole large enough for the insertion of the pipe.

Main and lower deck waterways with one or two exceptions do not vary greatly in type or arrangement. There may be either two or three strakes. In a two-strake waterway there will be the outer strake and the lock strake. In a three-strake water there will generally be one outer and one inner strake with a lock strake between them, though sometimes the lock strake is placed inboard with the other two strakes outside of it.

For the same reasons that outlines of the waterways were shown in connection with clamp and shelf details it has been considered necessary to show outlines of clamp and shelf details in these waterway details. It will be understood that no particular type of clamp or shelf arrangement is confined to use with a given type of waterways.

The width of the outer waterway strake or strakes must be such as to place the lock strake well in on the beam. The depth of the lock on the beam varies from two to three inches depending upon the size of the beam and waterways. The tops of waterways are generally made flush. The strakes are as a rule set square with the upper face of the beam, the outer strake being beveled to fay to the frames or stanchions.

Type 1, Fig. 132 shows a two-strake waterway as it would appear on the weather deck in way of the bulwarks and Fig. 133 shows the same type of waterway as it would appear either on a lower deck or on the weather deck in way of the bridge erection.

The space between the stanchions is chocked flush with the top of the waterways. These chocks should rest on the top timbers as shown in Fig. 132 and are usually fastened in place with hardwood treenails driven as shown. The inboard and outboard faces of these chocks should be exactly flush with the corresponding faces of the stanchions, and a calking seam should be provided at the ends and out-

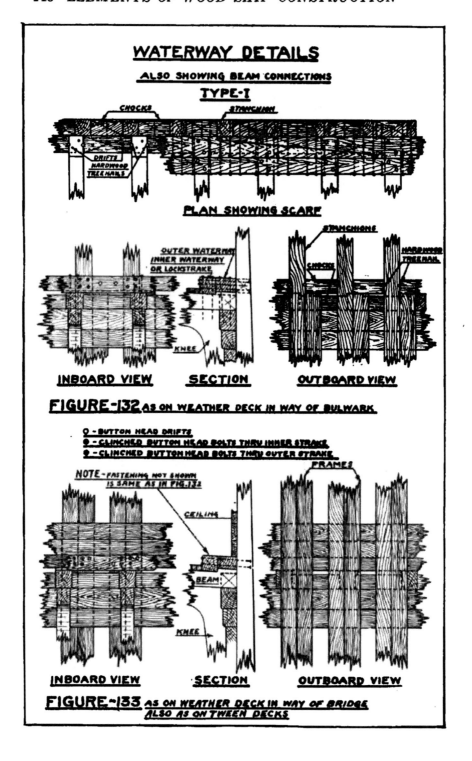

WATERWAY DETAILS

ALSO SHOWING BEAM CONNECTIONS

TYPE-I

PLAN SHOWING SCARF

INBOARD VIEW SECTION OUTBOARD VIEW

FIGURE-132 AS ON WEATHER DECK IN WAY OF BULWARK

○ - BUTTON HEAD DRIFTS
◑ - CLINCHED BUTTON HEAD BOLTS THRU INNER STRAKE
◐ - CLINCHED BUTTON HEAD BOLTS THRU OUTER STRAKE

NOTE-FASTENING NOT SHOWN IS SAME AS IN FIG.132

INBOARD VIEW SECTION OUTBOARD VIEW

FIGURE-133 AS ON WEATHER DECK IN WAY OF BRIDGE ALSO AS ON TWEEN DECKS

board face. The calking seam for the inboard face is generally run on the waterway strake.

Figure 132 also shows the proper setting of waterway scarfs. Nibs should be of standard depth and the scarf lengths should be extended beyond the standard if necessary to properly land the nibs. Calking seams must be run on the upper edges of all scarfs.

The most important part of waterway construction is the fastening. These members usually form one of the most important connections of the beams to the side of the ship and it is therefore essential that they be well and carefully fastened.

It will be noted that in this figure the outer strake receives two button-headed bolts driven from the outside and clinched over rings on the inside. The inner, or lock strake receives also two such bolts driven from the outside and clinched over rings on the inside. These four bolts are arranged to square up through the frame or stanchion. In addition two button-headed bolts are driven through both strakes into the chock, in way of the wells, and into the frame in way of the bridge where it is not necessary to fit chocks. For vertical fastening to the beam, each strake has two button-headed bolts driven at each beam, those in the outer strake extending into the clamps, and those in the lock strake being driven into the knee. Scarfs should have not less than two extra bolts between each frame or stanchion.

In Fig. 134 it will be seen that the fitting of shelves makes practically no difference in the number and location of the fastenings but does change the character of some of them. In this figure we have a typical three strake waterway and scarcely any comment need be made except to call attention to the vertical bolting of the lock and inner waterway strakes which, it will be seen, passes through the shelves and is clinched over rings below.

The foregoing descriptions apply to waterways as generally fitted on the main deck or decks below the main deck. When a shelter deck is to be fitted it may or may not be of lighter construction than the main deck. In small vessels it is generally made much lighter while in larger vessels the tendency is to make it even of heavier construction than the main deck. One type of waterway used in shelter decks of light construction is shown in Fig. 135. Here the waterway becomes nothing more or less than a covering board, and is worked and fastened as a covering board. This construction is not often used.

In Fig. 136 we have the waterway as applied to the bridge deck, and here as in Fig. 135 it is practically a covering board, and in fact is generally so called. The construction shown in this figure, including the waterway, clamps, and knee is practically typical for bridge decks, forecastle and poop decks.

On account of being in a location where there is great shrinkage these hanging knees are often fastened with screw bolts instead of the usual clinch bolts.

In either Fig. 135 or Fig. 136, the button-headed bolts fastening the waterway have the heads set down in counterbores which are plugged in the usual manner.

Figure 137 shows a patented arrangement of steel plates and hanging knees which is being used on a few ships in lieu of waterways and shelves or knees of wood. It is known as a reinforced construction. It may be noted here that this type of construction is used in connection with the diagonal planking system which has been mentioned before. Attention is called to the manner in which the chocks between the frames are dapped or dovetailed in place. These chocks are to receive the end fastening of the diagonal planking.

Figure 138 shows a typical arrangement of heavy scantling waterways and shelves for a shelter-decked vessel having two full decks and a lower tier of beams, known as lower, orlop, or hold beams. Note that the frames extend to the tops of the upper waterways, that the outer strake is dovetailed to the frame, and that the frame heads are covered with a planksheer. The fastening is not shown as there is nothing unusual in its arrangement.

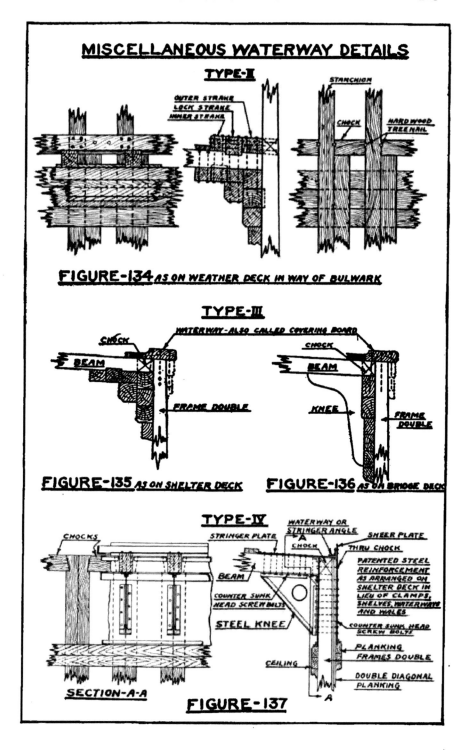

MISCELLANEOUS WATERWAY DETAILS

TYPE-I

OUTER STRAKE
LOCK STRAKE
INNER STRAKE

STANCHION
CHOCK
HARDWOOD TREENAIL

FIGURE-134 *AS ON WEATHER DECK IN WAY OF BULWARK*

TYPE-III

CHOCK
WATERWAY-ALSO CALLED COVERING BOARD
BEAM
FRAME DOUBLE

CHOCK
BEAM
KNEE
FRAME DOUBLE

FIGURE-135 *AS ON SHELTER DECK*   **FIGURE-136** *AS ON BRIDGE DECK*

TYPE-IV

CHOCKS

STRINGER PLATE
BEAM
COUNTER SUNK HEAD SCREW BOLTS
STEEL KNEE
CEILING

WATERWAY OR STRINGER ANGLE
CHOCK
SHEER PLATE
THRU CHOCK
PATENTED STEEL REINFORCEMENT AS ARRANGED ON SHELTER DECK IN LIEU OF CLAMPS, SHELVES, WATERWAYS AND WALES
COUNTER SUNK HEAD SCREW BOLTS
PLANKING
FRAMES DOUBLE
DOUBLE DIAGONAL PLANKING

SECTION-A-A

FIGURE-137

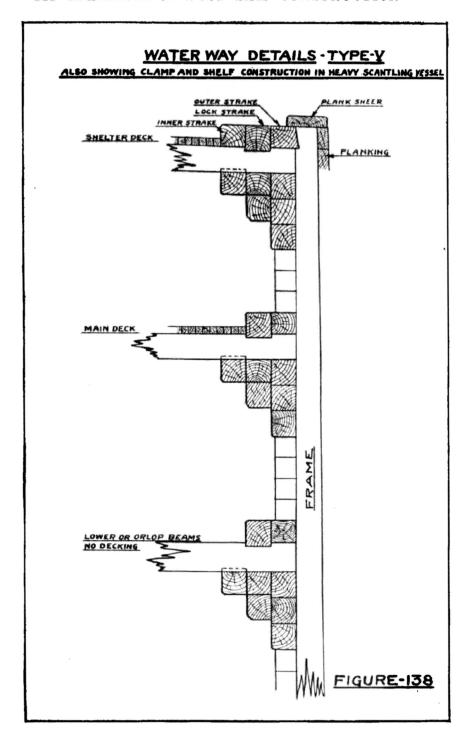

WATER WAY DETAILS - TYPE-V

ALSO SHOWING CLAMP AND SHELF CONSTRUCTION IN HEAVY SCANTLING VESSEL

FIGURE-138

Where waterways are extended to the stem, or around the stern, the various members have to be worked to shape as shown in Figs. 139 and 140. It will be noticed that not only is it necessary to use a close shift of scarfs at the ends of the vessel, but the scarfs are also shorter than the rule length. The shifts of scarfs that must be used are entirely dependent upon the curvature at the point where the timber is being fitted and the available width of the stock from which the timber is to be cut. Narrow stock will require close shifts of scarfs, and wide stock will permit greater shifts of scarfs, but there is a limit beyond which it is not wise to go even if very wide stock is available. This is due to the fact that where very wide stock is used to secure greater shifts of scarfs the result is often a scarf so cross grained that it has practically no strength. It is also to avoid this condition that scarfs are made shorter than the rule length.

In these figures two strakes of the waterways are shown carried to the stem and around the stern. Where a third waterway strake is fitted it is quite often stopped at the poop and forecastle bulkheads.

The lock strake, where carried around the stern, is made the same depth as the outer strake, that is, the lock is omitted in way of the rim.

The molds for the members to be worked to shape may be prepared in the loft, but should in any case be checked from the ship as some variations are bound to occur.

Where the stern is built up of solid work above the main deck there is no necessity of carrying the waterways around and they are generally allowed to run out against the solid work as shown by the dot and dash lines in Fig. 140.

At the stem in Fig. 139 a natural crook hook is fitted and fastened generally as shown in the figure. This hook has the same depth as the inner waterway strake, and the decking butts against it.

At the stern, where the two members of the inner strake butt at the centerline, an anchor stock is fitted, to avoid

10

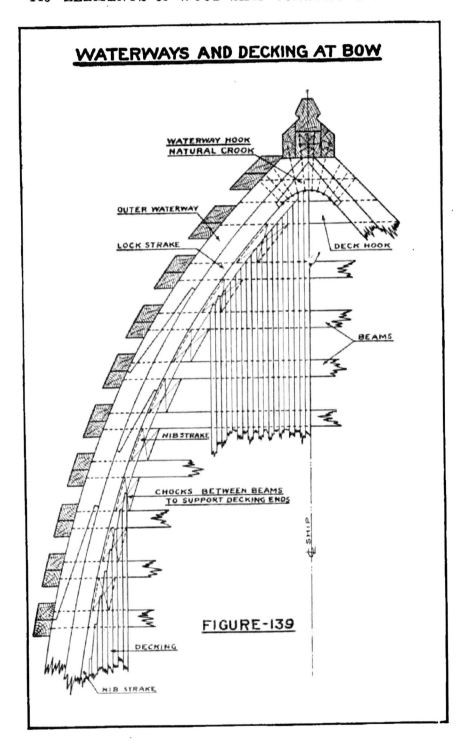

WATERWAYS AND DECKING AT BOW

WATERWAY HOOK
NATURAL CROOK

OUTER WATERWAY

LOCK STRAKE

DECK HOOK

BEAMS

NIB STRAKE

CHOCKS BETWEEN BEAMS
TO SUPPORT DECKING ENDS

⊄ SHIP

FIGURE-139

DECKING

NIB STRAKE

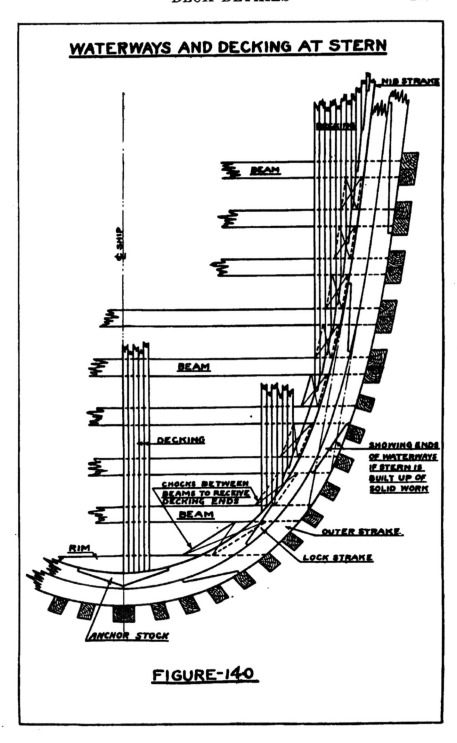

FIGURE-140

the excessive cross grain that would result with an ordinary scarf.

Both figures show clearly the chocks between the beams to receive the deck end fastenings and which have been previously mentioned.

The ends of decking should never be run off to a shim end where they land against the waterways, and a nib strake should be provided as shown in the figures. It will be seen that after the angle across the ends of the deck planks becomes rather blunt, the nib strake is either stopped as in Fig. 140 at the stern or merely has the deck plank butted against it as in Fig. 139 at the stem. Very often, however, at the bow the nibbing is carried to the end of the nib strake. There is no fixed rule for the angle across the deck ends at which the nibbing may be left off. However, in the author's opinion, nibs should be cut when the length of the cut across the end of the deck plank exceeds one and one half times the width of the plank.

Standard weather decking is generally square in section as shown in Fig. 141. The standard size is 4 inches by 4 inches, this being the net dimension as the decking is laid. Decking used on decks below the weather deck is often made thinner, and is also frequently made wider than its thickness.

To provide a good wearing surface all decking is invariably finished with vertical or edge grain showing on top face. The lumber from which it is made must be practically perfect.

It is customary to run the calking seam on each side of the deck plank as shown in Fig. 141. This is done at the mill. The total opening of the seam should not as a rule be greater than $\frac{1}{8}$ inch nor less than $\frac{1}{16}$ inch. General practice seems to favor an opening of about $\frac{3}{32}$ inch.

The customary minimum width of nib is shown in Fig. 143 and general arrangements of fastening are shown in Figs. 142 and 144. For the driving of the spikes used in deck fastening, a hole must be bored through the deck plank but not necessarily in the beam. The diameter of this hole is sometimes made the same size as the spike but the better practice seems to be to make it $\frac{1}{16}$ inch less, which provides for a slight drift of the spike through the plank. Sometimes when the holes are bored the latter size trouble is experienced by the decking splitting when the fastening is driven. This generally indicates either insufficient wedging of the plank or the use of a spike too large for the size of the decking. If the spike is too large a better job will be obtained by using a smaller spike which will permit the boring of the hole $\frac{1}{16}$ inch smaller in diameter than the size of the spike. As before mentioned no hole need be bored in the beam, but the spike must be so set that the chisel point will cut the grain of the wood in the beam.

A common rule for the size of deck spikes is $\frac{1}{8}$ inch square and two inches of length for each inch thickness of the deck plank. Thus, the spikes for decking four inches thick would be $\frac{1}{2}$ inch square and eight inches long. However, spikes of this size will very often give trouble by splitting the decking when they are driven in a $\frac{7}{16}$ inch diameter hole. It has also been demonstrated that they are unnecessarily long. Therefore the author commonly uses a spike $\frac{1}{16}$ inch less in square size, and one inch less in length than that given by the above rule. That is, the spike for four-inch decking would be $\frac{7}{16}$ inch square by seven inches in length and the hole through which it is driven would be $\frac{3}{8}$ inch in diameter.

Individual opinions upon these points differ, and as the size of spike to be used in any particular decking is always specified on the plans, it should where possible be used.

Spikes in the decking and similar locations are always set down in counterbores which are fitted with plugs of white pine or other similar wood as shown in Fig. 142. These counterbores are generally bored with special bits called plug bits, which are so constructed that they cut a perfectly clean hole of the exact size required. The depth of the counterbore should be gauged so that after

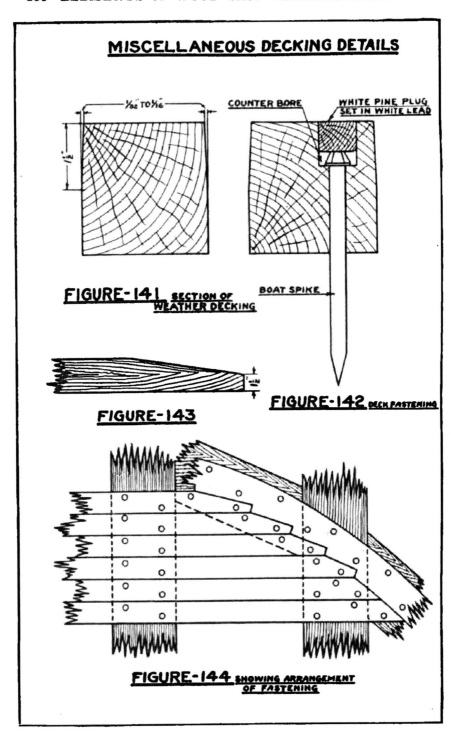

MISCELLANEOUS DECKING DETAILS

FIGURE-141 SECTION OF WEATHER DECKING

FIGURE-142 DECK FASTENING

FIGURE-143

FIGURE-144 SHOWING ARRANGEMENT OF FASTENING

the spike is set down snug there will be from ⅝ to ¾ inch of depth left for the plug. The plugs are then dipped in thick white lead and tapped down against the spike head. They should fit tight in the counterbores.

A common rule for the size of plugs is: Two times the diameter of the spike plus ⅛ inch. Thus, the diameter of plug for ½ inch spikes would be 1⅛ inch, and for a ⅜ inch spikes would be ⅞ inch, etc. Where spikes have extra large heads it may be necessary to add ⅛ inch to the size given by this rule.

HATCH DETAILS

In general, a hatch is any opening in the deck, rectangular in shape, and which is fitted with a coaming. They are framed in the deck for various purposes. A cargo hatch is for the loading and unloading of cargo. An engine hatch is framed to make way for the ship's engines and also to permit the shipping or unshipping of various portions of the engines in case of repairs and replacements. The boiler hatch bears the same relation to the boilers as does the engine hatch to the engines. There may be small hatches framed for no other purpose than to permit ingress or egress to and from a compartment, or they may be framed over the bunkers for coaling purposes, although for the latter, circular manholes with metal frames and covers are more often used.

Any hatch directly exposed to the weather must be fitted with covers and tarpaulins so fixed that water cannot gain admission to the hold. Cargo hatches in decks under the weather deck are commonly fitted with covers so that cargo may be stowed over the hatches, but they are not fitted with tarpaulins or made watertight.

Where any hatch is fitted with covers, the covers must be so supported that they will carry any load that may be placed upon them. In hatches below the weather deck this load is, of course, the weight of the cargo on top of the hatch covers. In the weather deck it may be either the weight of cargo or the weight of water that may by accident

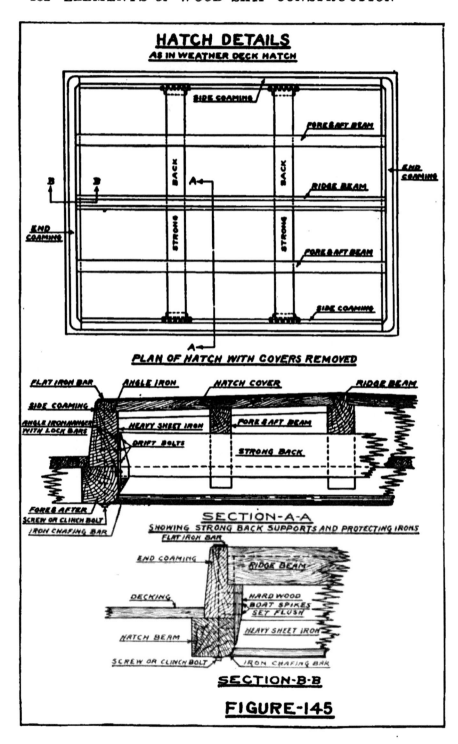

HATCH DETAILS

AS IN WEATHER DECK HATCH

PLAN OF HATCH WITH COVERS REMOVED

SECTION-A-A

SHOWING STRONG BACK SUPPORTS AND PROTECTING IRONS

SECTION-B-B

FIGURE-145

be taken aboard in a heavy sea, according to whether or not a deck load is carried. This requirement that the covers be strong enough to carry heavy loads, necessitates, in the case of large hatches such as cargo hatches, the fitting of a removable system of beams under the covers, one type of which has been detailed in Figs. 145 and 146.

There are a number of different arrangements of these beams in common use but they all consist essentially in a number of fore and aft beams having their ends supported at the coamings, with intermediate support furnished by thwartship beams called strongbacks, the ends of the latter being also supported at the coamings, and both the beams and strongbacks being removable. The number and size of beams and strongbacks to be fitted depend upon the size of the hatch and the load which they must carry. The end supports must be so arranged as to permit the ready shipping and unshipping of all beams and strongbacks, and at the same time must be strong enough to carry the load that may come upon them.

The center, or ridge beam, in weather deck hatches is generally rabbetted for the covers. In lower deck hatches the covers are more commonly butted together at the center as shown in Fig. 146.

Referring to Fig. 145 it will be seen that the ridge and fore and aft beams rest on top of the strongbacks, and that they are dapped at the ends into the coamings as far as the back of the rabbet. Since this depth of dap does not furnish bearing sufficient to support the beams hardwood wedges, as shown in Section B-B are fitted under each end of these beams. These wedges must be thoroughly fastened with either button-headed bolts or boat spikes. The strongbacks in this figure are supported in angle iron hangers set on the face of the coamings. It will be noted that these hangers are fastened with a large number of countersunk head drift bolts, and also that they have lock bars set into the wood to furnish the additional required bearing. Below the hangers it is customary to place small hardwood wedges to prevent the cargo tackle and blocks fouling on the hanger.

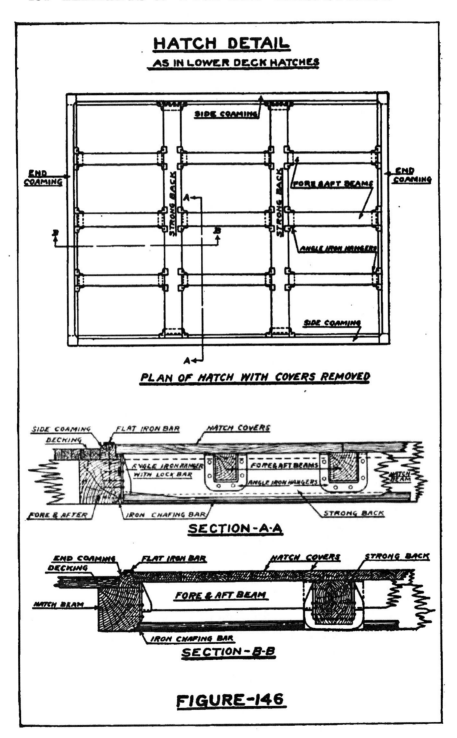

HATCH DETAIL

AS IN LOWER DECK HATCHES

PLAN OF HATCH WITH COVERS REMOVED

SECTION-A-A

SECTION-B-B

FIGURE-146

In Fig. 146, due to the smaller depth of the hatch, the beams and strongbacks must be set in the same line and all are supported by means of angle iron hangers. Here the fore and aft beams are not continuous but are cut in between the strongbacks. It should also be noted that the toes of the hangers are turned over at the top to furnish additional bearing to that given by the fastening, and that in addition to this the hangers for the strongbacks have one lock bar.

In many cases the angle iron hangers on the coamings are arranged to be set in flush with the face of the coaming, leaving these hatchways clear of all obstructions.

All exposed corners and wood surfaces on cargo hatches should be protected by iron work or sheathing. The entire inner face of the coamings and exposed hatch beams and fore and afters is generally lined with heavy sheet iron, or close spaced iron bars which should be fastened with either large wood screws or track spikes having countersunk heads. The rabbet should be protected with an angle iron and the lower inside corner with a quarter round chafing bar. Often the sheet iron sheathing is turned under the angle iron at the top and the chafing bar at the bottom. The tops of the coamings are generally protected with flat iron bars as shown in the figure. All of these irons may be properly called chafing irons. They should be fastened either with heavy wood screws or track spikes all of which should have countersunk heads.

HATCH COVERS AND MISCELLANEOUS

Hatch covers are generally built up of two planks edge bolted together as shown in Fig. 147. The total width of the cover depends upon the length of the hatch and the number of covers to be fitted, but it should not exceed 24 inches. Narrower widths are even better. Handholds are fitted at the two opposite corners of the cover. An enlarged detail of one style of handhold is shown in Fig. 148. No matter what style of handhold may be fitted it must in no case project above the surface of the hatch cover. The opening underneath the bar should be large enough to admit all of the fingers of an ordinary man's hand.

In addition, the hatch covers are numbered, generally with roman numerals cut in with a chisel, beginning with number one at the forward end of the hatch on each side. Since there will be two covers numbered one, and two numbered two, etc., they must in addition to the numbers have the letter P or the letter S cut on them, according as they belong on the port or starboard side of the hatch.

Weather deck hatches must be fitted with canvas tarpaulins to make them watertight. There are two general methods of fastening these tarpaulins in place which are shown in Figs. 149 and 150. In Fig. 149 the fastening consists of a line of cleats, usually cast steel, spaced from 18 to 24 inches apart around the hatch, and hatch battens of flat iron bars under which the tarpaulin is laid, the battens being secured with hardwood wedges driven in the jaws of the cleats as shown. Battens of hardwood may be used in place of the flat iron bar. In Fig. 150 a line of heavy staples, made usually of ⅝ inch diameter stock is set around the coamings at about the same spacing as would be used for cleats. A wood hatch batten is used on each side and end of the hatch, these battens being of hardwood and slotted to slip over the staples. The tarpaulin has grommets or eyes worked in it so that it also may be slipped over the staples. The wedges are half round in section and are driven through the opening of the staple.

Practice on large steamers seems to favor the cleat and iron or hardwood batten fastening as shown in Fig. 149. On small Pacific Coast steamers the staple and hardwood batten arrangement is quite generally used.

In addition to this fastening for the tarpaulins it is quite common to fit either two heavy iron straps or two wood beams over the tarpaulins to keep both the covers and tarpaulins down when the ship is pitching heavily as in a storm. These straps or beams extend fore and aft for the full length of the hatch, one being fitted on each side in line with the centers of the covers. They are securely fastened at the ends with bolts, fitted with handled nuts, the bolts being so arranged or hinged that they will drop out of the way when the hatches are open.

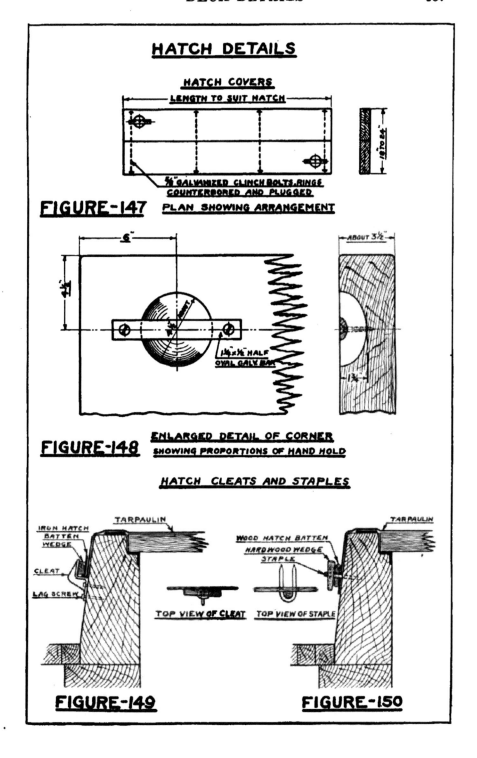

HATCH DETAILS

HATCH COVERS

FIGURE-147   PLAN SHOWING ARRANGEMENT

FIGURE-148   ENLARGED DETAIL OF CORNER
SHOWING PROPORTIONS OF HAND HOLD

HATCH CLEATS AND STAPLES

FIGURE-149   FIGURE-150

FOREWORD TO CHAPTER V

There are several special operations connected with ship work, particularly shipsmithing, sparmaking, and rigging, which will not be explained in detail, as they are highly specialized trades in themselves. Even though the iron work turned out by the shipsmiths, and the spars and rigging prepared by the sparmakers and riggers, generally require some woodwork preparation when they are fitted in place, it is usually of such simple nature as to require little or no comment here.

This final chapter takes up the problem of hull planking, and ends with a general discussion of joiner work. The previous chapter, it will be remembered, ended with the laying of the decking, and it has been mentioned that the planking of the hull would generally be under way at the same time. In fact, it is often started before any decking is laid, and in any case should be under way as soon as the ceiling has been completed.

The frames, as with the ceiling, must be dubbed fair so that the planks will fay properly to the timbers. Where no diagonal strapping or planking is used the dubbing is generally done at the same time as the planking, it being necessary only to keep the dubbers far enough ahead of the planking gang to be out of the way. But where the construction calls for either diagonal steel strapping, or diagonal planking, the entire frame should be dubbed fair before either is applied. And, of course, the planking proper cannot proceed until the diagonal stuff is in place. The only exception to this would be where the steel strapping ends at the heads of the floors in which case the garboards and some of the bottom planking may be run on while, or even before, the steel strapping is being placed.

Some portions of the hull erections may be completed

before the decking is laid, but the bulkheads enclosing them cannot be built until after the decking is laid. Hence it is quite common to leave all of these erections, with the exception of solid work around the stern, where used, until after the main deck has been completed.

As soon as the decks have been laid over the hull erections or, if there are no hull erections, as soon as the uppermost hull deck is laid, the joiner houses may be started. The completion of the joiner houses will in the main complete the construction work on the ship and it is at this point in most cases, assuming that the planking and calking has been completed that the ship is launched. Where work is being rushed, ships are frequently launched as soon as the planking and calking is finished, regardless of the work on the joiner houses since this work can be carried on after the ship is in the water.

Masts are generally not stepped until after the vessel has been launched and the setting up of the rigging which has been previously prepared by the riggers naturally follows the stepping of the masts. It is the best practice to have the upper ends of the standing rigging attached to the masts before they are stepped.

There are many items of equipment which may or may not be placed upon the ship before launching. Ironwork such as the stem iron, side, or cheek plates on the stern- and rudder-posts, arch reinforcing plates, and similar details should all be in place before launching. Likewise all sea chests should be complete and fitted with strainers and valves. All bollards, chocks, mooring rings, hawse pipes, etc., should be in their places, and properly fastened, so that means will be provided for attaching lines or cables for checking the headway of the vessel after it leaves the ways during launching, and for mooring to the dock of outfitting pier later on. Loose equipment, and boiler and engine-room equipment including the boilers, main propelling engines and auxiliaries, are not generally installed until after the vessel is in the water. The propeller and tail shaft, with its bearings, are often shipped while the vessel is still on the stocks and this, where possible, is most desirable as it saves docking the vessel to ship these items.

Rudders, whether of wood or steel, are more readily shipped when the vessel is still on the stocks, but if so shipped they must be very strongly shored in the midship, or fore and aft, position to prevent their swinging about and doing damage not only to the rudder itself, but the ship as well, during launching.

During the stages of construction covered in this chapter, the order of procedure depends largely upon the order in which materials and outfit are supplied to the yard. It is also often a matter of choice or custom on the part of the yard management. This applies particularly to the state of completion at which the vessel may be launched. While in most localities the vessel is launched in a more or less uncompleted condition, in some it has been the custom to launch vessels, particularly sailing vessels, complete, with all rigging and equipment, ready for the sea. Steamers are seldom held on the stocks until completed in every respect.

Since the order of procedure may vary considerably the tabulation as given in other chapters is omitted.

CHAPTER V

PLANKING, ERECTIONS AND JOINER WORK

DIAGONAL STRAPPING AND PLANKING]

Large vessels must be reinforced with either diagonal iron strapping, or diagonal planking. While both of these arrangements are quite old, the use of diagonal planking did not until quite recently come into favor.

Both systems are applied directly on the outside of the frames. For either to be efficient and accomplish the purpose for which it is intended, requires extreme care in fitting so that fair contact with the frames is secured at all points.

Diagonal iron strapping generally consists of a wide band, set at or slightly below the sheer line, extending from approximately abreast the stern post to a short distance abaft the stem. As shown in Fig. 151 the diagonal straps are attached to this band and so arranged that they cross in the frame bays, where they are riveted to each other. Both the straps and the wide plate at the top are dapped into the frames so that their outer surfaces do not extend outside the fair surface of the frames. Each strap is fastened at each frame with at least one countersunk head drift bolt, the best arrangement being to stagger these on the frames as shown in the figure. If two bolts are driven to each frame the stagger rule will of course not hold good.

The diagonal straps should extend downward around the bilge and onto the ends, or heads, of the floors at least 24 inches, where they should be extra fastened.

Around the bilge they are often set or dapped in deep enough to permit dubbing the frame flat under each strake of planking which saves the expense of hollowing out the faying surface of the planking to fit a rounded bilge. As has been mentioned before, it is best where possible to do the dubbing before the strapping is fitted, as then there is no uncertainty about how deep the strapping must be

11   161

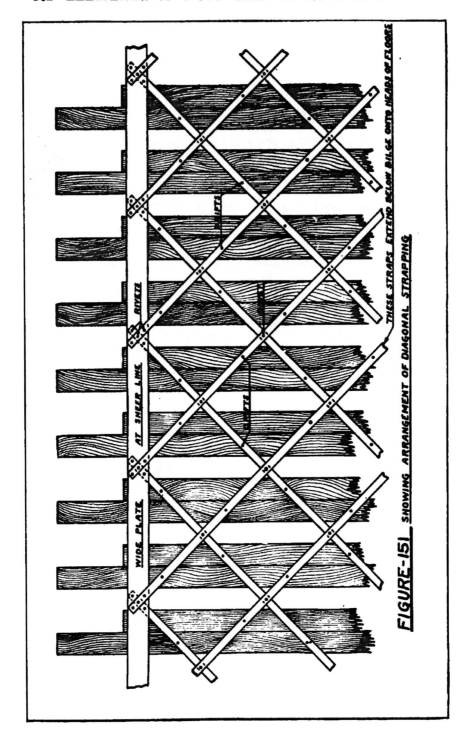

FIGURE-151 SHOWING ARRANGEMENT OF DIAGONAL STRAPPING

dapped into the frame to clear the planking. The daps should not be deeper than absolutely necessary as they in any case tend to weaken the frame.

Diagonal planking, or sheathing as it is sometimes called, is laid in two courses, each course being at an angle of about 45 degrees to the keel and about square with the other course. It covers the entire frame of the vessel from stem to stern. The frame bays at the tops and along the keel are chocked to provide continuous fastening surface for the upper and lower ends of the diagonal stuff. This chocking has been shown in previous figures.

At the ends of the ship, separate rabbets are cut for the diagonal planking where possible so that the end fastening of the diagonals will not land in way of the hood end fastening of the outside planking. Along the keel, and above the shaft log at the stern there is generally but one rabbet for both the diagonal and outside planking.

As before explained, the entire frame of the vessel must be dubbed fair before diagonal planking can be applied.

It is customary to start the diagonal planking at a point near midship, working thence each way to the ends of the ship. While the planking as started should be at an angle of 45 degrees with the keel, it will be found as the work progresses fore and aft, that one edge will buck up, or refuse to fay to the frame, around the bilge when the plank is bent to place. This is due to the shape of the ship and the greater distance from end to end of the vessel around the frame at the top than along the keel, which soon causes the upper ends of the diagonals to fall behind the lower ends. When this point is reached it is necessary to take off what is known as a spiling. This is done by springing a thin wood batten about $\frac{3}{8}$ inch thick and 6 inches wide, around the frames in the position of the next strake of planking to be fitted. This batten, known as a spiling batten, is allowed to lay in its natural position, and the amount that it springs away from the edge of the last strake of planking will indicate the taper that must be cut on the next strake to correct the work. At some points in the ship it may be necessary to take a spiling every fifth or sixth strake. The operation of spiling is explained in detail further on in this chapter.

The diagonal planking is fastened with common galvanized wire nails just sufficient to hold it up against the frames until the outside planking is put on. The nails for the first course are generally shorter than those driven in the second course, each being of such length as to penetrate the frame for about the same distance. They are driven at the extreme outer edge of the frames so as not to interfere with the planking fastening. This arrangement of the fastening also serves to mark out the location of the frames which have now been completely covered up. In addition to this, however, the locations of the edges of all timbers in the frames should be accurately scribed on the outside of the diagonal planking, so that the outside plank fastening may be properly located.

HULL PLANKING

The most important single operation in connection with the planking is without doubt the lining. Upon the man who does this work, called the liner, depends not only the ease or difficulty as the case may be with which the planking goes on, but very often the neat and shipshape appearance of the vessel itself. Poor lining will make hard planking and in addition generally spoils the appearance of the vessel through having seams running in unfair lines.

For the purpose of illustration a definite problem has been assumed.

The first step in lining is the selection of the frame having the greatest girth from keel rabbet to the uppermost deck line. This is often done on the loft floor, in which case the strakes of planking may then be laid out full size on the selected frame as shown in Fig. 152. This figure shows the frame of greatest girth in a shelter deck vessel, and it will be noted that the uppermost strake, called the sheer strake, is above the deck line, and is not treated as a strake of planking. It would therefore be without taper fore and aft. If, however, it is desired to taper the sheer strake in the same proportion as the other planking it should be figured in the girth.

It should be further noted that this figure shows diagonal planking. If diagonal strapping is used the planks would be laid off on the frame proper. The widths are laid off on the outside of the planking.

Planking in general may be divided into two groups. The first would be the bottom planking, including the garboards, the strakes of which are run either with no taper or an irregular taper, and which are called here untapered planking. The second group, comprising the balance of the hull planking is generally run with a uniform taper, and is here called tapered planking. The point where the change is made from the untapered to the tapered planking is largely a matter of choice and judgment with the liner, and cannot be definitely fixed by any rule. In this problem all of the garboard and bottom plank are considered as untapered and they occupy 190 inches of the total girth of 624 inches leaving 434 inches for the tapered strakes. This, of course, at the greatest girth.

Having laid out the planking as above indicated, and tentatively fixed the point of change from the untapered to the tapered planking, the liner will then estimate the amount of room required by the tapered planking at the ends of ship.

Generally, tapered strakes may have a total taper from their widest point to the ends of the ship of from 1½ to 3 inches depending upon the shape of the hull. The taper at the stem, will as a rule be less than that at the extreme stern, but will probably be more than the taper measured at a point abreast the stern post. In this problem it is assumed that the liner has tentatively decided upon a minimum width of 5½ inches at the stem and 6¼ inches abreast the stern post, for the 7½ inch strakes. Since all of the tapered planking is assumed to have a uniform taper, or percentage of taper, the corresponding width of the entire

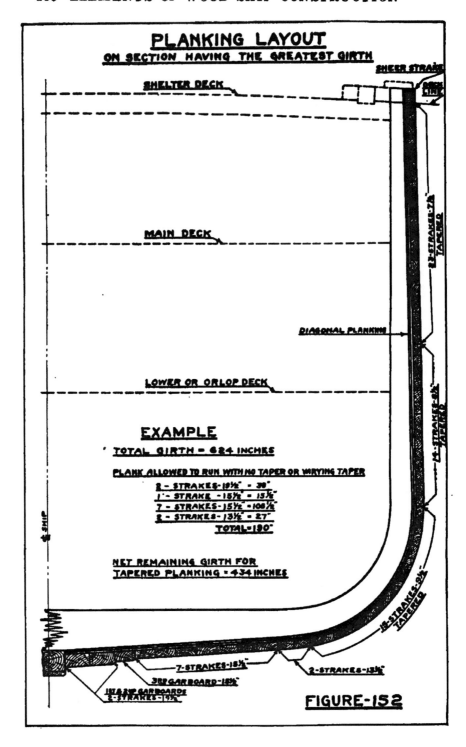

PLANKING LAYOUT

ON SECTION HAVING THE GREATEST GIRTH

SHEER STRAKE

SHELTER DECK

MAIN DECK

DIAGONAL PLANKING

LOWER OR ORLOP DECK

EXAMPLE

TOTAL GIRTH = 624 INCHES

PLANK ALLOWED TO RUN WITH NO TAPER OR VARYING TAPER

2 - STRAKES- 19½" - 39"
1 - STRAKE - 15½" - 15½"
7 - STRAKES- 15½" - 108½"
2 - STRAKES- 13½" - 27"
TOTAL=190"

NET REMAINING GIRTH FOR
TAPERED PLANKING = 434 INCHES

FIGURE-152

belt of tapered planking at the two points may be quickly estimated.

Now, 5½ inches are roughly 73 percent of 7½ inches and 6¼ inches are roughly 83 percent of 7½ inches. The the total girth occupied by the tapered strakes in Fig. 152, the widest point, is 434 inches. Seventy-three percent of 434 inches is approximately 316 inches, hence with the above assumed taper the lower edge of the tapered planking would land 316 inches down from the deck line at the stem. Again, 83 percent of 434 inches is approximately 360 inches, and this would be the distance down from the deck line abreast the stern post for the lower edge of the taper planking.

If, after measuring 316 inches down from the deck line at the stem, the remaining distance to top of the keel, is 190 inches or less the taper assumed forward may generally be used. The distance remaining to the top of the keel at the stern post after measuring 360 inches down from the deck line, may very likely be more than 190 inches, which will not indicate that the taper cannot be used, but that a stealer, or possibly more than one, will have to be fitted as shown in Fig. 153. The amount of taper which can, or should, be used on the tapered planking at the stern depends greatly upon the shape of the stern. Very often it is necessary to bring the planking lines up to the tuck very sharply, in order that the tapered plank above may not have too much edge set, and in such cases the liner may disregard the tapered planking at the stern until such time as he sees that the planking will run fair into the tuck on a natural line— a natural line being one that requires little or no edge setting of the plank.

Having established the points at the stem and the stern post which he will attempt to reach with the untapered planking the liner will proceed to run in the garboards and bottom planking, lining, or laying out, each strake individually on the frames. He will in all probability spile the garboard hoods, to throw their upper edges on a more natural line. The balance of the strakes included in untapered planking he will either run with slight taper, no taper, or with stealers as may be required to reach the point where the tapered planking can begin. Each strake will be so lined as to keep it in the most natural position and for that reason they will most likely vary considerable in taper at the ends. Spilings will be taken only where absolutely necessary. After the untapered planking is all on, the line where the taper planking begins should be practically a natural line. The planking will then be at the stage shown in Fig. 153.

The frequent adjustments of taper necessary to keep the untapered planking near natural lines will in all probability prevent the liner exactly reaching the original points selected on the stem and stern post. In this problem it is assumed that the remaining girth for tapered planking, at the stem is 312 inches and at the stern post 352 inches, which it will be seen are somewhat less than the original girths decided upon. It is also assumed here that the tapered planking begins on the same strake at the stem and stern, but this is by no means an invariable rule. Quite frequently the shape of the stern will require a different number of tapered strakes from that used at the stem. The principles of determining the taper, however, remain the same.

Girths for tapered planking must now be measured at frequent intervals as shown in Fig. 154. The number of girths shown here is suitable for small boats only. In large vessels a greater number should be taken. It is not necessary to take them at even intervals as shown. In fact an experienced liner will check girths wherever he suspects there is a necessity for so doing, keeping a record of them by merely noting the frame numbers at which they were measured. For the purposes of this problem they have been numbered from one to six. The girths as measured may be set down in a table as shown in Fig. 155.

Now, the widths of the strakes at the greatest girth of 434 inches are 9½, 8½, and 7½ inches respectively. To

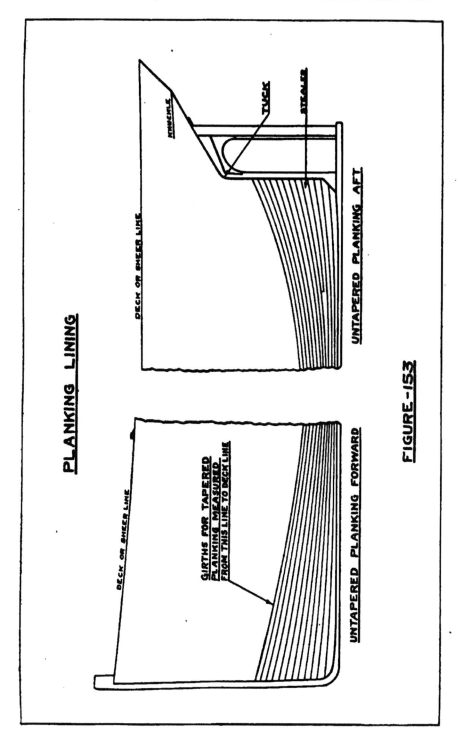

PLANKING LINING

DECK OR SHEER LINE

KNUCKLE

TUCK

STEALER

UNTAPERED PLANKING AFT

DECK OR SHEER LINE

GIRTHS FOR TAPERED PLANKING MEASURED FROM THIS LINE TO DECK LINE

UNTAPERED PLANKING FORWARD

FIGURE - 153

PLANKING LINING

EXAMPLE SAME AS IN FIGURE-152

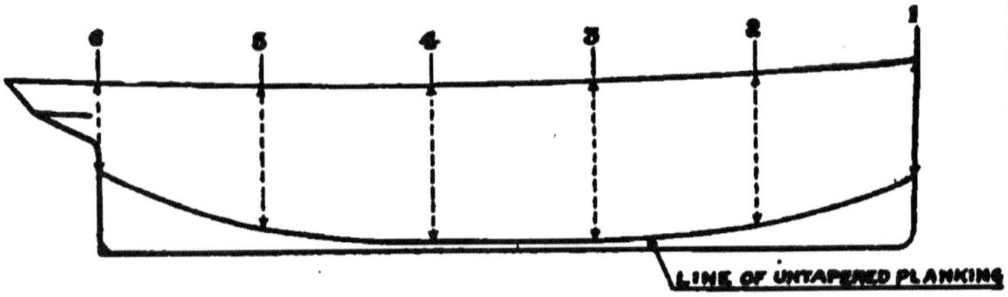

LINE OF UNTAPERED PLANKING

FIGURE-154 GIRTHS

GIRTH TABLE

No.1	312 INCHES
No.2	376 INCHES
No.3	434 INCHES
No.4	424 INCHES
No.5	392 INCHES
No.6	352 INCHES

FIGURE-155

PLANKING AT GIRTH N⁰3

15 - STRAKES - 9½" - 142½ INCHES
14 - STRAKES - 8½" - 119 INCHES
23 - STRAKES - 7½" - 172½ INCHES
TOTAL 434 - INCHES

FIGURE-156

TABULATION OF PLANK WIDTHS AT ALL GIRTHS

STRAKES	GIRTH N⁰1	GIRTH N⁰2	GIRTH N⁰3	GIRTH N⁰4	GIRTH N⁰5	GIRTH N⁰6
7½"	5⁹⁄₃₂"	6½"	7½"	7⁵⁄₃₂"	6¹¹⁄₃₂"	6¾₂"
8½"	6⅛"	7⅛"	8½"	8⁵⁄₁₆"	7¹⁄₁₆"	6½₂"
9½"	6⁶⁄₃₂"	8¼"	9½"	9¹⁄₃₂"	8⁵⁄₃₂"	7¹⁵⁄₃₂"

FIGURE-157

GRAPHIC METHOD OF FINDING PLANK TAPERS

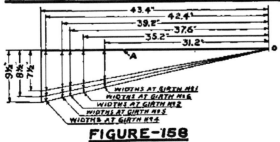

FIGURE-158

find the required width at any other girth less than the greatest girth it is only necessary to find the percentage that the lesser girth bears to the greatest girth, then this same percentage of the width of the strake at the greatest girth will give the required width at the lesser girth. This operation may be set down as follows:

Required: Width of strakes at girth No. 2.
Greatest girth equals 434 inches.
Girth No. 2 equals 376 inches.
376 is 86.7 per cent. of 434.
Then 86.7 per cent. of 7½ inches equals 6½ inches.
86.7 per cent. of 8½ inches equals 7⅜ inches.
86.7 per cent. of 9½ inches equals 8¼ inches.

and 6½, 7⅜, and 8¼ inches will be the required widths of planking at girth No. 2. A like calculation is made for each girth less than the greatest girth. It will be easier for some to set the calculation down in the following form:

$$\frac{376 \times 15}{434 \times 2} = 6\tfrac{1}{2} \text{ inches.}$$

$$\frac{376 \times 17}{434 \times 2} = 7\tfrac{3}{8} \text{ inches.}$$

$$\frac{376 \times 19}{434 \times 2} = 8\tfrac{1}{4} \text{ inches.}$$

After the widths are calculated for each girth they may be tabulated as shown in Fig. 157. The widths are here given to the nearest ⅟₃₂ inch.

Figure 158 shows a graphic method of determining the required planking widths at the various girths without any calculation whatever, which is laid out as follows:

On the straight line A measure from the point O one-tenth (one-twentieth would do as well) of each girth and from each point so measured draw a line down and square from the line A. On the last line so drawn measure down from line A the widths of planking at the greatest girth, and join each of the points thus measured to O with a straight line. This completes the figure, and the required widths of the 7½-inch strakes at all girths may be directly measured from line A to the line drawn from O to the 7½ mark, these measurements being taken on the lines previously squared down from the line A at the points representing the lengths of the various girths, as shown by the arrow heads in the figure. Likewise the required widths of the 8½- and 9½-inch strakes may be taken directly from the figure.

Tapered planking is not generally spiled, as it is usually of such narrow widths as to easily take the required edge set.

It is customary to plank first from the keel to a point above the turn of the bilge, and then plank from the deck line down to this point, the last strake placed being known as the shutter. Thus, if any unfairness in planking lines develops as the tapered planking is run on, the correcting strakes will be located at or below the water line, near the shutter, and will not spoil the appearance of the job. Sometimes two planking gangs are worked at the same time, one working from the bottom up, and the other working from the top down, in which case, if the tapered planking is started before the untapered is finished, it is run in on estimated tapers at the top, the correction strakes being located in the vicinity of the shutter.

It is seldom that any two liners will approach the lining problem in exactly the same manner, and for this reason no two will arrive at exactly the same result in the finished job, either in the respective number of tapered and untapered strakes used, or the amount of taper on the tapered planking.

SPILING

Spiling battens may be used to determine the shape of either one or both edges of a plank and the principles of taking the spiling are the same in each case.

Fore and after hoods of the first garboard strakes are generally ordered wider than the balance of the strakes so that they may be spiled to fit. If this was not done it would not only require very heavy edge set to bring the hood ends down to the rabbets, but would throw a hump in the planking edge abaft the stem and forward of the stern post that would increase the difficulty of setting the next strake.

One method of taking a garboard forehood spiling is detailed in Figs. 159 and 160. The liner first runs in the line of the upper edge of the garboard, being careful to keep within the limits required by the available width of stock ordered for this piece. A thin wide spiling batten is then roughed out to clear both the rabbets and the line, and tacked in its natural position, as shown in the figure.

Then set a compass, or divider, at such radius as to permit the scribing of a good portion of a circle on the batten when the center point is held on either the line of the upper edge of the garboard or the inner rabbet line. With the compass or divider so set, scribe arcs on the batten as shown in the figure, at frequent intervals. Where the curvature is sharp they should be scribed very close together.

The batten is next taken off the ship and laid on the timber from which the forehood is to be cut. If the forehood is to be fitted without edge set the batten will be permitted to lay in its natural position in marking out the piece. If, however, the top edge of the garboard is to be left straight, it is most likely that the forward end of the batten will have to be sprung up to fit it. The amount of spring necessary to make the batten fit the straight upper edge of the hood will be the same as the amount of edge set required to fit the forehood in place on the ship if the upper edge is left straight. If this is excessive in the opinion of the liner some of the spring is taken out of the batten, and the upper edge of the garboard will then be cut with some curvature.

To scribe the points off the batten onto the hood timber, the compasses or dividers are used with the same radius as when the batten was scribed from the ship, the center point being set first at one point on the arc, then at another point about 90 degrees from the first, and short arcs drawn so that they will cross as shown in the figure. When the batten is sprung up to fit the straight upper edge of the garboard, the arcs at the top must cross directly on the edge

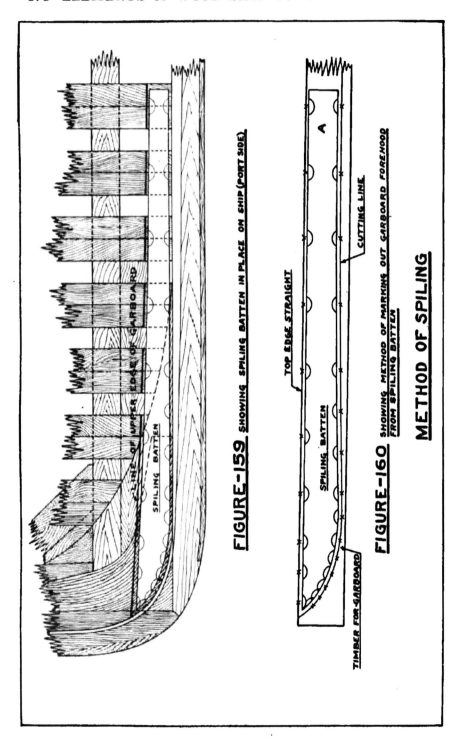

FIGURE-159 SHOWING SPILING BATTEN IN PLACE ON SHIP (PORT SIDE)

FIGURE-160 SHOWING METHOD OF MARKING OUT GARBOARD FOREHOOD FROM SPILING BATTEN

METHOD OF SPILING

of the timber. The balance of the points are then marked off with the batten held in this position. It will thus be seen that with the same spiling batten, it is possible to lay out the garboard forehood with either no edge set, or the full edge set required by leaving the upper edge of the garboard straight, or any intermediate desired edge set, according to the conditions, width of available stock, and the liners judgment.

The after end of the batten should in any of the above conditions, be placed on the timber so that its upper scribe marks fit, or are parallel to, the upper edge of the timber. This end is then held in this position whether or not the forward end is sprung from its natural position. The width of the garboard at the point A is also generally made the same as the balance of the strake.

It should be noted in Fig. 160 that the cutting line indicates the shape of the faying side of the hood to fit the inner rabbet, and that, as the batten is scribed, the cutting line will appear on the outer face of the hood. The rabbet bevels therefore have to be taken and proper allowance made for them in establishing the corrected cutting line. The corrected line will generally be slightly outside of the first scribed line, the bevels reading under so that after the hood is cut, the lower inner corner will correspond to the first scribed line and will fit the inner rabbet. The bevels are taken in much the same manner as ceiling bevels, except that a calking seam is provided. This simply means that the bevel run on the edge of the hood is slightly less than that taken from the rabbet.

The rabbet on the keel, as it approaches the stem and stern post is gradually reduced, or tapered, in its depth, so that at the stem and stern post it will be only as deep as required by the top side planking. Hence fore and after hoods of the garboards must in all cases be tapered off in thickness to fit the rabbet. Since the after end of the fore hood and the fore end of the after hood must be the same thickness as the balance of the strake amidships, there is often a great deal of material to be taken off in thinning the hood ends. Very often the taper in thickness is cut with as much twist as the original thickness of the timber will permit, this twist being in the direction that the hood will have to be twisted in forcing it to its place. This reduces the amount of twist that the timber must stand and decreases by that much the difficulty of getting the hoods in place.

All planking which has to be bent, twisted, or edge set must be thoroughly steamed.

The bevels for the edges of the planking may in general be lifted in the same manner as has been p eviously described for ceiling bevels, except that it will not be found necessary to reverse them to obtain a surface for scribing the cutting line. This may be explained another way by stating that wherever the extreme breadth of either ceiling or planking is utilized, the bevels as taken from the ship must be converted into standing bevels, or the cutting line would appear on the extreme edge of the timber and could not be defined. Since planking bevels as taken from the ship are already standing, or where under, are at a point not using the full width of the plank, it is not necessary to reverse them.

The allowance for the calking seam is generally made when the bevels are lifted from the ship. It is customary in most yards to allow an opening not to exceed ⅛ inch at the outside face of the planking.

PLANK FASTENINGS

Number and arrangement of fastenings for planks from 5 to 16 inches in width are shown in Fig. 161. It should be noted that two spikes count as one fastening.

As a rule, the number of fastenings to be driven is regulated by the width of the plank, while the diameter is regulated by the thickness of the plank, and the material of the fastening. It is also customary in some localities to keep the diameter of the largest fastening down to about one-eighth the siding of the frame timbers, which in some cases might require an increase of the number to be driven.

PLANK FASTENINGS

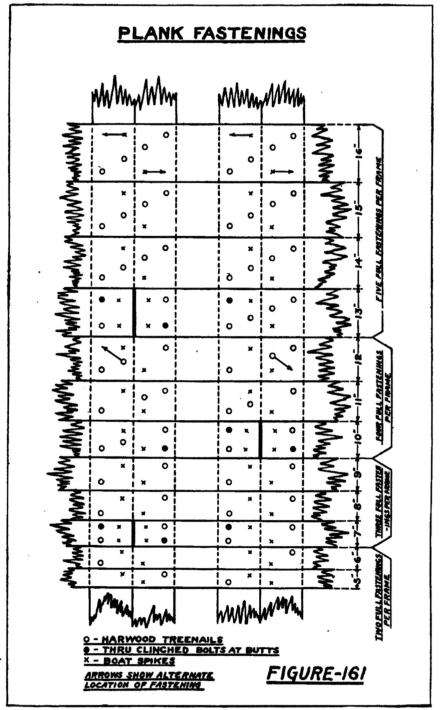

O - HARWOOD TREENAILS
● - THRU CLINCHED BOLTS AT BUTTS
X - BOAT SPIKES
ARROWS SHOW ALTERNATE
LOCATION OF FASTENING

FIGURE-161

Hardwood treenails, are generally made from selected black locust, and may vary in diameter as driven from $1\frac{1}{4}$ inches to $1\frac{1}{2}$ inches, depending upon the thickness of the planking. All treenails, where possible are driven through the ceiling inside, then cut off flush on both ends and wedged with small oak wedges made for that purpose and called treenail wedges. The wedges must be set across the grain of the plank through which the treenail is driven. Where treenails are not driven through, a wedge is inserted in the end of the treenail which, when the treenail is driven, backs up against the bottom of the hole and wedges the treenail fast.

There are three general types of treenails in use. The first is straight, and is driven in a hole about $\frac{1}{16}$ inch smaller than the treenail. When it is necessary to drive treenails of this type longer than about 24 inches, it becomes rather difficult to get them in with the proper amount of drift. Hence a second type has been devised where about one-half of the length of the treenail is sized about $\frac{1}{8}$ inch smaller than the other half. These are driven in holes bored first about half-way through the hull with an auger $\frac{1}{16}$ smaller than the large end of the treenail, and the rest of the way with an auger $\frac{1}{16}$ smaller than the small part of the treenail. This in effect shortens the required length of drift and makes it possible to drive much longer treenails than would be the case with the first type. Such treenails are known as two-drift treenails. The third type is tapered and is driven in a two size hole bored in the same manner as described for the two-drift treenails. The large end of the treenail is about $\frac{1}{8}$ inch larger than the larger portion of the hole, while the small end is the same size as the smaller portion of the hole. It is claimed that these treenails when driven properly cannot be backed out and that they actually hold the planking up against the frame.

All holes are bored, and all treenails are driven, from the outside.

In some instances button-headed bolts have been sub-stituted for treenails, the same number being driven, and about one-half of them driven through the ceiling inside and clinched over rings.

The spike fastening is commonly known as the working fastening, as it is used to hold the plank in place until the planking gang can get clear for the fastening gang. It will be noted that two spikes are driven to each frame in Fig. 161 for all widths of planking. This is a maximum number and very often fastening arrangements call for not more than one spike to the frame.

The size of the spike is regulated by the thickness of the plank, the old rule being—$\frac{1}{8}$ inch square and 2 inches long for each inch thickness of plank. Thus a spike for 5-inch planking would be $\frac{5}{8}$ inch square and 10 inches long. Another rule adds one inch to the length thus ob-tained. Where the vessel has diagonal planking, the thick-ness of this must also be added to the length as obtained by the above rule.

Each plank butt must be extra fastened with two button-headed bolts, driven through and clinched over rings inside the ceiling. These may be arranged as shown in the figure.

Alternate arrangements of some of the fastenings are shown by arrows. The arrangement shown here is but one of several in use, and where plans show detail fastening arrangements, they should of course be carefully followed.

The shift of butts shown in Fig. 161, is the minimum customarily permitted, and where possible greater shifts should be used. The rule for minimum shifts may be stated as follows:

Butts in adjoining strakes shall have three frame spaces between. Butts in the next strake but one, shall have two frame spaces between. Butts in the next strake but two shall have one frame space between (as shown in the figure). Butts in the next strake but three may land on the same frame, or butts landing on the same frame shall have three strakes between. Butts shall not be arranged in even sequence or steps.

The above shift of butts will, with a frame spacing of three feet, require an average length of planking of only about 36 feet, hence it will be seen that it can easily be maintained in any locality, and very much bettered where long timber is available.

HULL ERECTIONS

Hull erections include any erection on the hull proper which extends above the main rail. They are sometimes called deck erections, but since this latter term is also applied to the joiner houses, it is deemed best to here differentiate between the two. In general hull erections will include the poop, bridge, and forecastle, the bridge being located amidships. Sometimes the bridge is set further aft and combined with the poop, making what is known as a long connecting poop and bridge. Figure 194 shows the location of these structures on a vessel of the Three Island Type.

There are two general methods of building up that portion of the poop rounding the stern. The first is by the use of swinging cants set around the stern, these extending to the poop deck, as has been shown in the chapter on framing. The usual planking on the sides of the poop is then run around the stern and there is no solid work.

In the second method, the after portion of the poop is built up entirely of solid work, as shown in Figs. 162 and 163. Figure 162 shows a construction quite commonly used on small vessels built on the Pacific Coast, and is shown here for comparison with the construction detailed in Fig. 163 which is used on larger vessels. In Fig. 162 it will be noted that the solid work around the stern carries the same detail as the bulwark which is shown in Section A-A. Owing to the fact that the bulwark planking is quite narrow, one course of solid work is made to represent two bulwark planks by cutting a V groove in the middle of the course.

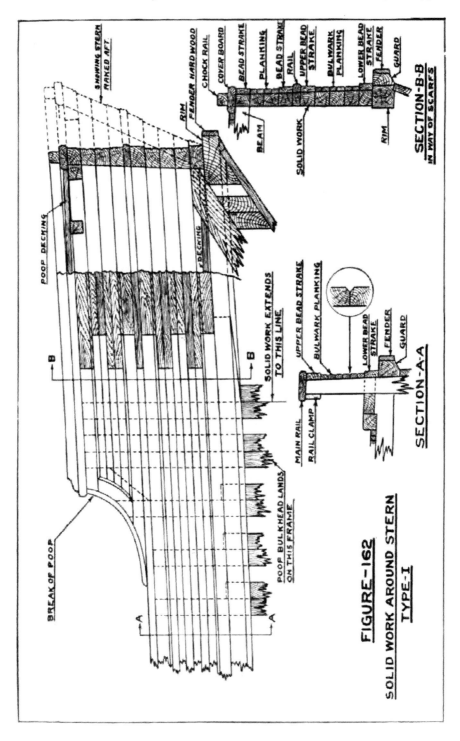

FIGURE-162

SOLID WORK AROUND STERN
TYPE-I

The courses should where possible match up with the seams in the bulwark and poop planking as shown in the figure. Where the seams of the solid work are not made to fair into seams of the bulwark and poop planking, it is necessary to wedge them flush and cut V grooves to fair with the corresponding V grooves in the planking seams.

This type of solid work is molded the same as the thickness of the planking, plus the molding of the frame, hence the inside face of this work, where it butts against the first frame extending to the poop deck, will be exactly flush with the inside of the frame. It is customary to carry this same molding around the stern. The type of stern on which this solid work is used, has been shown in Fig. 64, and by referring to this figure it will be seen that the rim lands on top of the after timber of the frame against which the solid work ends, and that the solid work will therefore extend to the center-line of the frame and abut the forward timber.

The bulwark planking and side planking of the poop must be scarfed back onto the solid work. In order to break the scarfs and avoid what would appear to be a vertical seam at this point, about one-half of the planks are scarfed back further than the balance as shown in the figure. The solid work showing on the outside is grained in the figure to make it stand out from the planking. A section through the scarfs is shown at B-B. Comparison of this section with that of the bulwark will show that the outside detail has been retained exactly. The rail clamp, and that portion of the main rail extending inside the inner face of the stanchion has been stopped at the poop bulkhead.

There are several variations of the construction shown in this figure which can and have been used. In the most notable one, where the poop is short, the main rail is extended through as a solid course, all frames being stopped against it as in a bulwark, and all work above the main rail to the break is solid work, of the same type as here shown further aft. The solid work however carries the same detail as shown in the figure.

The type of solid work shown in Fig. 163 is the same as that indicated on the stern frame shown in Fig. 66 Chapter II, where it will be noted that the rim sets some distance above the deck line. The bulwark detail as shown in Section A-A is not carried around the stern but is returned at a point about in line with the break of the poop. To accomplish this return the butt joints between the thin bulwark planking and the heavier strakes on each side and those extending to the stern, are arranged on the curve indicated in the figure. Then the beading is cut on the ends of the heavier strakes, around this curve, care being taken to have it exactly match and fair into the beading on the upper and lower bead strakes.

The solid work in this figure has a sharp rake aft at the extreme after end. This rake gradually diminishes toward the sides of the poop until at the section B-B it will disappear and the work will be practically plumb. Forward of the point where the section B-B is taken it may have a slight tumble home.

The sides of the poop are planked, this being scarfed back onto the solid work as shown. Since the outside surfaces are finished flush, without V grooves for trim, no attempt is made to have the seams of the planking and solid work match up. Where this can be done however it would probably result in improved appearance as the vessel gets older and the seams tend to open up and show.

The outside face of this rim is faired to the outer face of the planking. The forward ends abut the frame and the outer portion, corresponding to the plank, or knuckle strake is carried to the center of the frame, to make a proper butt against the knuckle strake. The knuckle strake (shown shaded), is fitted to fair out the knuckle line forward of the rim, to a fair planking surface, as the rim is so short that it is generally impossible to fair out the knuckle line, or make it disappear, on the rim proper. The forward end of the knuckle strake will be the same as a plank, while the after end will match the rim.

Since the main rail is not carried around the stern it is

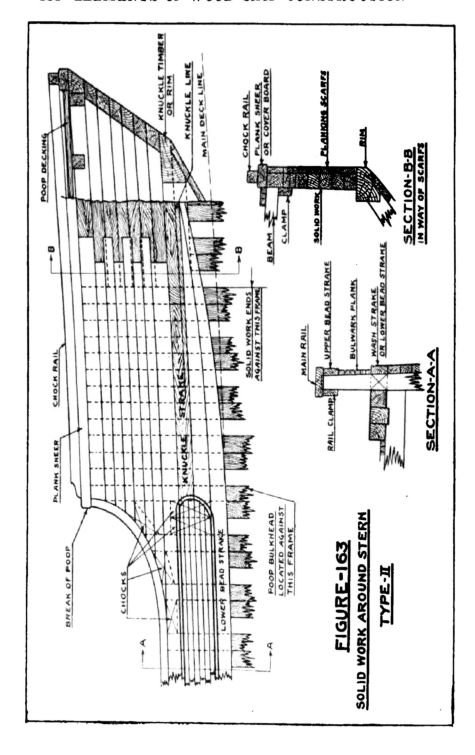

FIGURE-163
SOLID WORK AROUND STERN
TYPE-II

necessary to either stop it off short, forward of the break of the poop, or carry it up to the poop deck as shown in the figure. The latter arrangement gives the best appearance. The curved portion of the rail is sawn to actual shape, and should be in short sections to avoid undue cross grain.

Molds for the timber comprising the solid work may be lifted course by course from the ship, or from the loft floor. If lifted from the loft floor, the sawing must be very carefully done to avoid hollow places which cannot be dressed, or joinered out. As put in place they are generally rough sawn, the dressing, or joinering being done afterwards.

It should be noted in connection with all of these erections, that the planking, bead strakes, etc., above the main deck, or upper deck line, are run without taper, the one exception being, in Fig. 163 at the stern where the planks below the bead strake, and which are still above the deck line have to be treated as hull planks, and are therefore tapered.

Solid work is generally butted square and the butts may be arranged as shown in Fig. 165. Where the main rail is carried solid without break around the stern, as was explained in the discussion of Fig. 162 it is customary to scarf all of the rail butts in the manner shown in Fig. 164, except at the forward ends, where of course the rail would continue forward unbroken. Where solid work butts are scarfed the arrangement would generally be as shown in the figure.

The common fastening arrangement for solid work is shown in Fig. 165. All bolts are drifts, driven blunt. The arrangement shown is subject to modification as may be required by the particular arrangement of the work.

Figure 166 shows a quite common arrangement of planking on the sides of the forecastle. The bulwark planking is returned just aft of the hawse pipe hole. Above the main rail course there is a panel of thin planking having the sam thickness as the bulwark planking, which is returned a little further forward than the bulwark planking. These

ARRANGEMENT OF SCARFS

WHERE USED IN SOLID WORK
COVERING BOARDS, CHOCK RAILS OR
OTHER HEAVY STRAKES AROUND STERN

EXAMPLE AS IN SOLID WORK

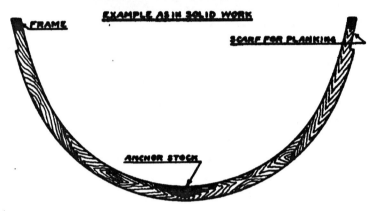

FRAME

SCARF FOR PLANKING

ANCHOR STOCK

FIGURE-164

ARRANGEMENT OF BUTTS
AND FASTENING
IN SOLID WORK AROUND STERN

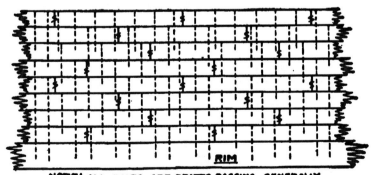

RIM

NOTE! ALL BOLTS ARE DRIFTS PASSING GENERALLY
THRU TWO AND ONE HALF STRAKES OR COURSES

FIGURE-165

returns at this point are necessary because all planking entering the rabbet in this vicinity must be the same thickness. If the thin planking were continued to the rabbet, it would be necessary to cut the rabbet further aft on the stem than the rabbet for the thick planking shows, or if carried to the same rabbet a portion of the rabbet would show outside of the planking. Either arrangement would leave an unsightly job. There is a method, where the thin planking extends over the whole side of the forecastle, of running it to the same rabbet. This is done by either leaving the frames next to the stem full on the outer face, or shimming them out, so as to throw the outside face of the thin planking at the rabbet flush with the outside face of the thick planking. The rabbet for the thinner planking is then cut from the same outside rabbet line, but only to the depth required by the thinner planking, thus leaving an unbroken exterior. This method is often used to avoid the return above the main rail course, in which case the strakes corresponding to the bead strakes above the main rail course would be left without the beading, and would be tapered at the rabbet to the thickness of the thin planking.

Monkey rails, where fitted, are usually built up of solid work as shown in the figure and fastened in the same manner as described for solid work at the stern.

The frames in way of the bridge erection are extended to the bridge deck in the same manner as shown at the forecastle. The outside planking detail may vary somewhat but in general, very much the same detail of thin strakes, bead strakes, etc., will be used as have been shown for the end erections. If a panel is used above the main rail in way of the bridge, it will be returned at each end in the same manner as shown at the break of the forecastle in Fig. 166. The bulwark planking is generally carried through without break.

The hull erections are generally ceiled inside with thin ceiling from the waterways to the clamps. Very often tongue and groove stuff is used. Clamps should be fitted for landing the beams, and they are fastened very much as hull clamps.

It is customary in many yards, to saw the poop and forecastle beams with the full camber on the top face, leaving the bottom face straight. However where the arrangement of interior bulkheads permits they may be, and often are, sprung in the same manner as hull beams are sprung. Beams for bridge erections generally have the same partial camber sawn on both upper and under sides, the balance being sprung. Hull erection beams are generally fitted with hanging knees, it being the best practice to fit one to each beam end in way of the bridge, and three or four on each side of the poop or forecastle as may be required.

The common arrangement of coverboard, or covering board, scarfs around the after end of the poop is the same as that shown in Fig. 164. On the forecastle it will also be necessary to scarf in the coverboard in relatively short lengths, and the scarfs may be arranged in the same form as has been previously shown in connection with the waterways at this point.

Against the apron, or stem, if there is no apron at this point, there should be a deck hook, in way of the forecastle beams. The coverboard should also be fitted with a natural crook hook cut to the same shape as waterway hooks, and well fastened. There should be a stout breast hook set just under, or even with the top of the small rail on top of the monkey rail, this being well fastened through the monkey rail and to the stem.

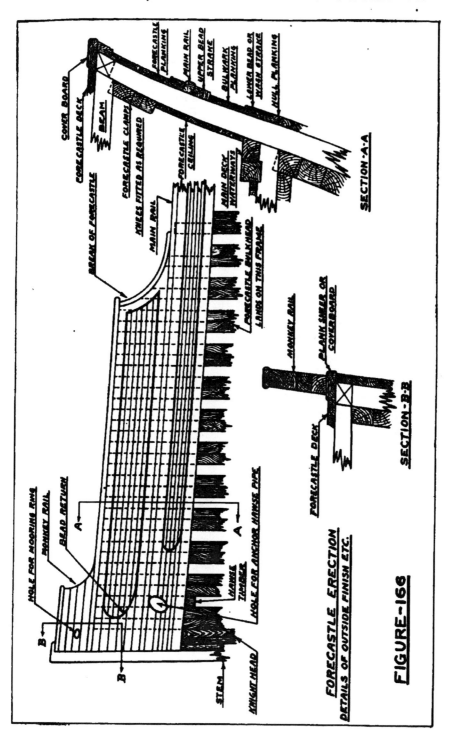

FORECASTLE ERECTION
DETAILS OF OUTSIDE FINISH ETC.

FIGURE-166

MAIN RAIL

The main rail has already been mentioned but only in a general way. In ordinary types of ship construction this member forms one of the principal upper strength members, and is therefore carefully fitted and fastened. It should be in very long lengths, with scarfs of standard or longer length, set on edge, with standard nibs, and thoroughly edge bolted in the manner shown in Fig. 167. These scarfs are quite frequently made with a hook.

The fastening is generally by button-headed bolts driven into the stanchion head, rail clamp, and bead strake, and arranged as shown in the figure. To render this fastening effective the clamp is generally through clinch fastened to the bead strake, the common arrangement being two spikes for working fastening, and two clinched bolts to each stanchion, the bolts being button headed and driven from the outside. The main rail fastening is set down in counterbores, which are plugged.

Very often the main rail is mortised about one inch over the heads of the stanchions, but this must be very carefully done to be of any real value to the work.

The special type of bulwark in Fig. 168 is shown here for the interest it may have for the reader in making comparisons between the different types of construction prevailing. It is a modification of the type of steel reinforcement that has been previously shown for shelter deck vessels. One of the principal points of interest is the fact that the main rail in reality consists of a steel plate set over the stanchion heads, and that the main rail, so called in the figure, acts principally as a fender for this plate.

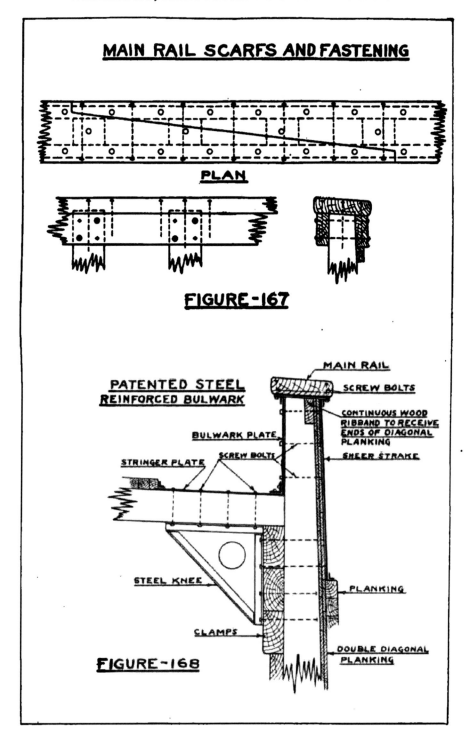

MAIN RAIL SCARFS AND FASTENING

PLAN

FIGURE -167

PATENTED STEEL
REINFORCED BULWARK

MAIN RAIL

SCREW BOLTS

CONTINUOUS WOOD
RIBBAND TO RECEIVE
ENDS OF DIAGONAL
PLANKING

BULWARK PLATE

SCREW BOLTS

SHEER STRAKE

STRINGER PLATE

STEEL KNEE

PLANKING

CLAMPS

FIGURE-168

DOUBLE DIAGONAL
PLANKING

SCUPPERS AND FREEING PORTS

Scuppers must be provided in all hull weather decks. Freeing ports are required in all bulwarks in way of wells, on account of the larger quantity of water from which it may be necessary to free the deck.

A section showing a deck scupper as quite commonly cut, is shown in Fig. 169. The hole is oval in shape and is lined with heavy lead flanged over on the wood at each end and fastened with copper nails. Strainers are often fitted on the inner end, but are not so necessary where the opening stands on edge as in the figure. Extra chocks should be fitted where such scuppers are cut so that the lead will be supported for its full length.

On small western steamers the freeing ports are often arranged as shown at Type A in the same figure. It will be seen that they consist of openings formed by cutting out sections of the first bulwark strake above the head strake. In vessels, where the lower edge of the head strake is set even with the top of the waterways, the openings are cut in the lower half of the head strake. They are not fitted with hinged covers, and will of course admit water as well as let it out from the spaces enclosed by the bulwark.

The type of freeing port most generally favored consists of a large opening cut in the bulwark as shown at Type B. This opening is fitted with a metal cover hinged at the top, so that it will swing outward only. This arrangement will permit large quantities of water to flow from the decks enclosed by the bulwarks, but will permit very little to flow into these spaces, should the port be submerged. The total area of freeing ports required on any ship is fixed by the rules of the Classification Society under which the vessel is to be classed.

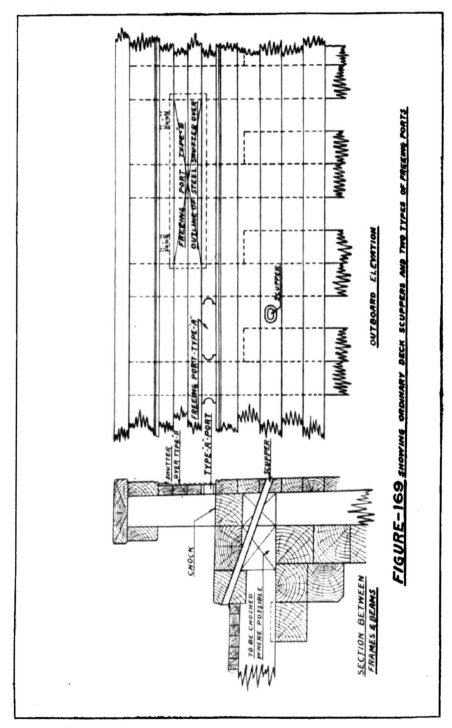

FIGURE-169 *SHOWING ORDINARY DECK SCUPPERS AND TWO TYPES OF FREEING PORTS*

MAST COLLARS, WEDGES AND STEPS

Where masts pass through decks they are fitted with hardwood collars and wedges arranged generally as shown in Fig. 170. The collar is made up of from four to six pieces, or segments, and is scribed down through the decking to the beams and partners. The collar is fitted before the mast is stepped, then the hole is carefully lined and trimmed to the proper size and taper for the wedges. The method of lining has been previously explained. The taper on the wedges may vary somewhat but should not be less than ½ inch to the foot. The wedges are made longer than finally required, and after the mast has been stepped and secured in its proper position, they are carefully driven down hard as far as they will go, then trimmed off even at the top. After this work has been completed, a petticoat, or boot, as it is also called, of heavy canvas is fitted around the mast and to the deck to make the job watertight.

Mast steps should always be of hardwood, and well fastened in place. The mortise of mast to step is frequently made of the common blind type as has been shown on stern posts. The form of mortise shown in Fig. 171 while rather complicated, is designed to secure the greatest possible strength in the thwartship direction.

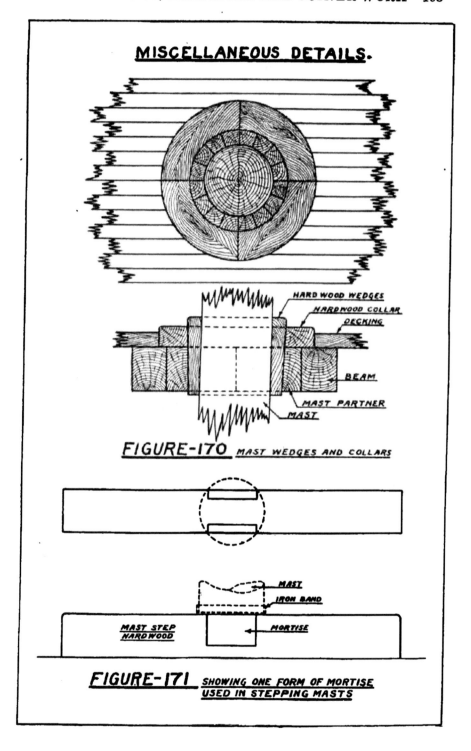

MISCELLANEOUS DETAILS.

HARD WOOD WEDGES
HARDWOOD COLLAR
DECKING
BEAM
MAST PARTNER
MAST

FIGURE-170 MAST WEDGES AND COLLARS

MAST
IRON BAND
MAST STEP HARDWOOD
MORTISE

FIGURE-171 SHOWING ONE FORM OF MORTISE USED IN STEPPING MASTS

JOINER WORK

Joiner work in general includes all houses above the bridge, or shelter decks, also all subdividing bulkheads, or partitions in the poop and forecastle compartments, as well as any erection, or housing that may be required above either the poop or forecastle decks. While the work may vary greatly in detail design in different localities, and yards, the principles of construction used are very much the same.

The details shown in this chapter, in Figs. 172 to 193 inclusive are for the main part taken from one type of design, and the reader may therefore note that while the arrangement of the named items existing in any particular ship house will very closely follow that shown in the figures, the shape or design of such parts, or items, may, without causing the work to be less attractive, or substantial, be quite different. For this reason, the discussion here on this work will be quite general, and no attempt will be made to describe each plate in detail, except where the construction shown seems to call for explanation.

Figure 172 shows one of several types of construction for bulkheads at the ends of poop, bridge, and forecastle erections. These bulkheads must be very strong and watertight.

Since they are liable to receive severe shocks when water is taken on board in a storm at sea, the ordinary type of mortise for the studding is not considered strong enough in most cases. It is therefore customary to use some such construction as shown in the figure, to develop the full strength of the stud at the upper and lower ends.

The coamings, both outside and inside are scribed to the shape of the deck, being worked from timber wide enough for this purpose. The outer coaming is frequently but not always cut down into the decking as shown in the figure to provide a better calking seam than would result with the coaming simply fayed on top of the decking. This

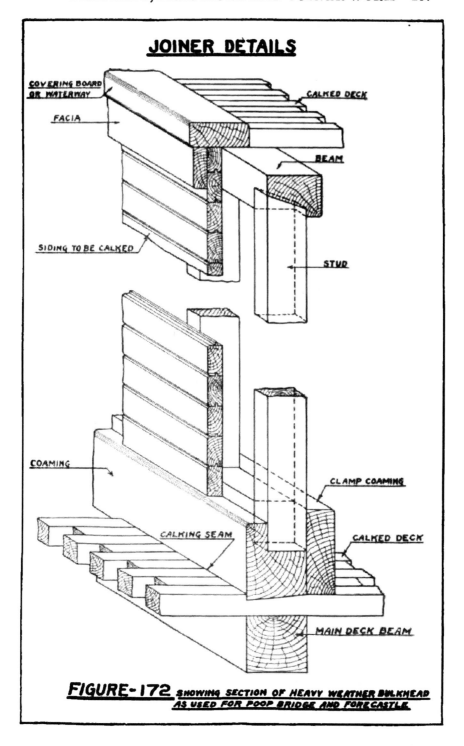

JOINER DETAILS

COVERING BOARD OR WATERWAY

CALKED DECK

FACIA

BEAM

SIDING TO BE CALKED

STUD

COAMING

CLAMP COAMING

CALKING SEAM

CALKED DECK

MAIN DECK BEAM

FIGURE-172 SHOWING SECTION OF HEAVY WEATHER BULKHEAD AS USED FOR POOP BRIDGE AND FORECASTLE.

arrangement, while giving a better calking seam, weakens the decking and is therefore open to objection.

The studding is very heavy and is spaced at close intervals. The siding, or planking, may be as shown in the figure, or there may be an inner diagonal course of thinner planks, with an outside course of either special shiplap, or matched stuff, both courses being, on the outside of the studding.

Doors fitted to these bulkheads are generally of special construction, and so fitted as to be watertight.

The is some confusion in the use of the terms coaming, and sill as applied to joiner work. In general the coaming is a rather high, rabbeted member, set either on top of the decking or on the beams, to which the studs are mortised, and which is exposed to the weather. It therefore would appear only at the exterior of the houses, or erections. A similar member, in the interior, fitted always on top of the decking, and at the bottom of bulkheads, or partitions, is generally called a sill.

Figures 173 and 174 show coaming details as commonly used on houses built on calked decks. The fore and aft coamings, as shown in Fig. 173 are set on the beams, and it will be noted that at the ends of the houses they are cut down to the thickness of the deck planking and carried to the center of the next beam. This is to avoid the fitting of a chock between the beams to receive the fastening of the decking ends landing against the end of the coaming, should it be cut off at the corner. Particular note should be taken of the shape of the rabbet across the corner and the corresponding shape of the foot of the corner post shown in Fig. 179.

Figures 175 and 176 show details of coamings as generally fitted on joiner decks. They are as a rule, not so high as the coamings used on bridge decks and they set on top of the decking, both at the sides and ends of the houses. In other respects they are much the same as the higher coamings shown in Figs. 173 and 174.

Thwartship coamings, where too heavy to permit

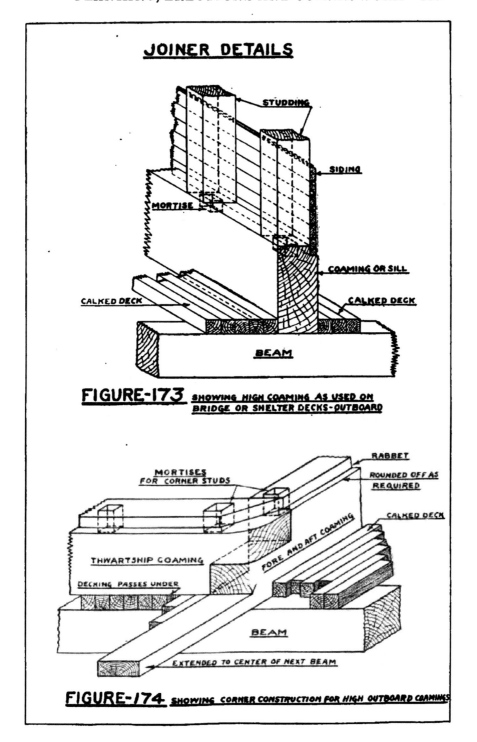

JOINER DETAILS

STUDDING

SIDING

MORTISE

COAMING OR SILL

CALKED DECK

CALKED DECK

BEAM

FIGURE-173 SHOWING HIGH COAMING AS USED ON BRIDGE OR SHELTER DECKS-OUTBOARD

MORTISES FOR CORNER STUDS

RABBET

ROUNDED OFF AS REQUIRED

CALKED DECK

FORE AND AFT COAMING

THWARTSHIP COAMING

DECKING PASSES UNDER

BEAM

EXTENDED TO CENTER OF NEXT BEAM

FIGURE-174 SHOWING CORNER CONSTRUCTION FOR HIGH OUTBOARD COAMINGS

springing must be scribed from wider timber to the shape, or camber, of the deck. All coamings, whether on calked or joiner decks, should be thoroughly fastened with either screw or clinched bolts, preferably the former, passing through the beams, with nuts set up below on large washers.

Figure 175 shows the deck canvas turned up against the coaming. In some yards it is the custom to lay the deck canvas before any coamings or sills are placed, in which case the coamings would be on top of the canvas. So long as the canvas is carefully laid, and the joint against the coaming made watertight by close tacking and paying with white lead, there is no relative advantage in either arrangement.

It is customary to lay canvas over a layer of tarred felt, but of late, practice in this respect has altered, the canvas being laid directly to the deck, after the latter has received a priming coat of paint prepared specially for this purpose. The felt, where used, should not be tacked.

Corner post details, together with the corner studding, plate, and end beam, are shown in Figs. 177 to 180 inclusive. It should be noted that the corner post is, in a measure, a false member, in that it is so arranged that it can be slipped into place after the corner studding, plate and end beam are set up. The siding and ceiling are nailed to both the corner studs and post.

As a rule, the light beams used in houses are called carlines. The heavier members over the studding at the ends are called end beams. Reference may also be made at this time to the different terms used for siding and ceiling. While the term ceiling is almost universally used to designate the inside sheathing, the outer sheathing, is often called simply sheathing instead of siding. Since there may be in special cases diagonal sheathing under the siding, it is deemed best to use the term siding here in referring to the horizontal matched finish on the outside of the houses.

Siding and ceiling as used on merchant vessels consists generally of plain V groove matched lumber.

Inboard bulkheads, or partitions, in joiner house may be either built on studding, as shown in Fig. 181, or they

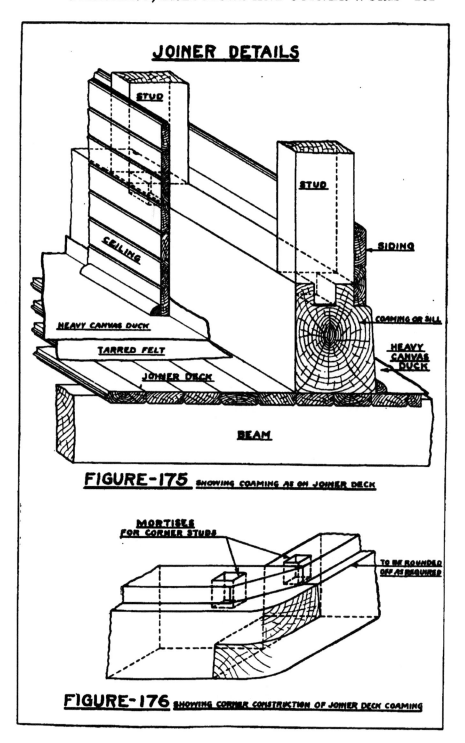

JOINER DETAILS

STUD

STUD

CEILING

SIDING

HEAVY CANVAS DUCK

TARRED FELT

JOINER DECK

COAMING OR SILL

HEAVY CANVAS DUCK

BEAM

FIGURE-175 SHOWING COAMING AS ON JOINER DECK

MORTISES FOR CORNER STUDS

TO BE ROUNDED OFF AS REQUIRED

FIGURE-176 SHOWING CORNER CONSTRUCTION OF JOINER DECK COAMING

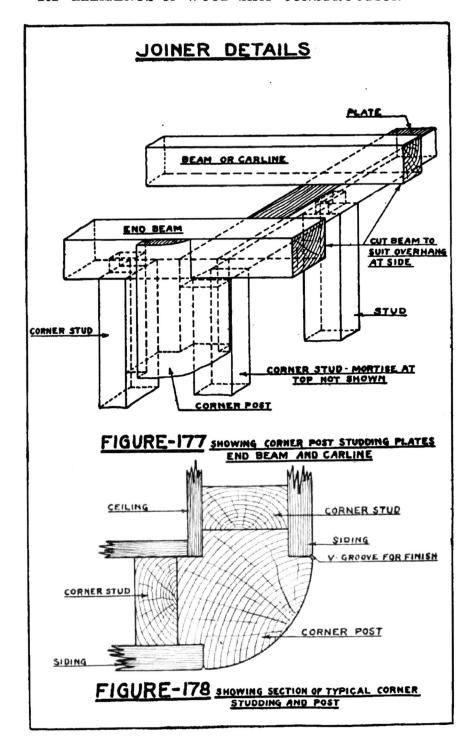

JOINER DETAILS

FIGURE-177 SHOWING CORNER POST STUDDING PLATES END BEAM AND CARLINE

FIGURE-178 SHOWING SECTION OF TYPICAL CORNER STUDDING AND POST

may be built up of two thicknesses of ceiling, one thickness set vertical, and the other set diagonal, at an angle of about 45 degrees, the two thicknesses being well fastened together. The latter construction is called a diagonal bulkhead. Where diagonal bulkheads are longer than about 8 feet they should be fitted with wide spaced studs sufficient to stiffen the bulkhead as required. The edges of these bulkheads are landed in special moldings or nailing strips, which are first well fastened in place. If the bulkhead lands on a carline, the two courses are either run up the side of the carline, or rabbetted into it, and the nailing strip is not used.

Before the siding and ceiling are placed on the outside walls, or bulkheads of the houses, the holding down rods must be fitted. These should be spaced as shown on the joiner plans, or if not shown on the plans, at sufficiently close intervals to securely hold the plates and end beams down against the studding. They should pass through the plate, or end beam, coaming, deck, and beam, or carline, underneath. They are generally made up from galvanized or composition rods, with nuts and washers at both top and bottom, and should be set up perfectly tight before any of the siding or trim is placed.

Two types of door trim are shown in Figs. 182, 183, and 187. Type I, Figs. 182 and 183, is quite generally used for both outside and inside doors, but the construction shown in Type II, Fig. 187, is considered to be the better arrangement for outside, or weather doors. With the type of trim shown in Figs. 182 and 183, the joint between head and side jambs is frequently made in the manner shown in Fig. 184. If not made in this manner, it would in any case show a miter at the edges, the middle part being coped. The side jamb is coped over the threshold in such manner that the threshold may be set in place first, and the balance of the frame slipped into place over it. In Fig. 187 the outside part of the jambs would be mitered at the top, while the main pieces would show a miter inside to the rabbet, the balance being coped. The main piece sets

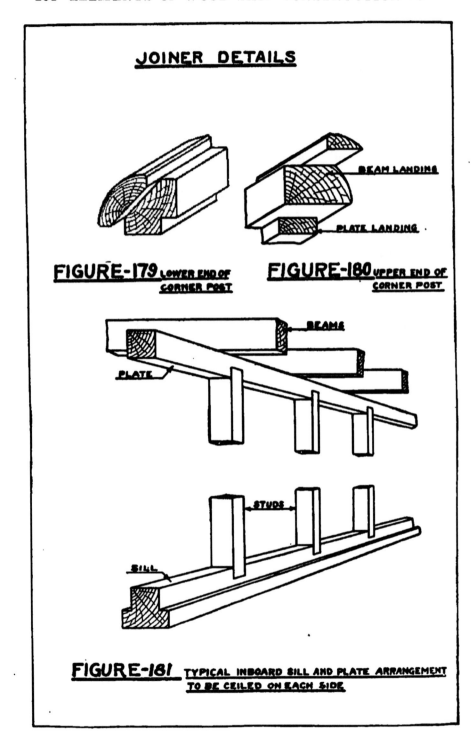

JOINER DETAILS

FIGURE-179 LOWER END OF CORNER POST

FIGURE-180 UPPER END OF CORNER POST

BEAM LANDING

PLATE LANDING

BEAMS

PLATE

STUDS

SILL

FIGURE-181 TYPICAL INBOARD SILL AND PLATE ARRANGEMENT TO BE CEILED ON EACH SIDE

JOINER DETAILS

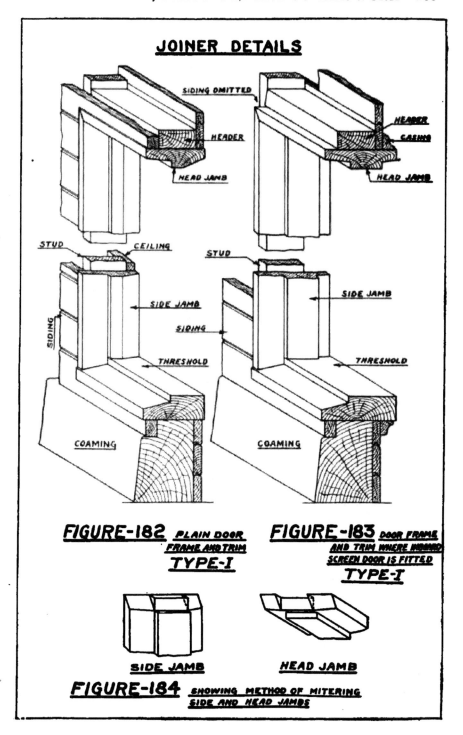

SIDING OMITTED

HEADER

HEAD JAMB

HEADER

CASING

HEAD JAMB

STUD

CEILING

STUD

SIDE JAMB

SIDE JAMB

SIDING

SIDING

THRESHOLD

THRESHOLD

COAMING

COAMING

FIGURE-182 *PLAIN DOOR FRAME AND TRIM*
TYPE-I

FIGURE-183 *DOOR FRAME AND TRIM WHERE INBOARD SCREEN DOOR IS FITTED*
TYPE-I

SIDE JAMB

HEAD JAMB

FIGURE-184 *SHOWING METHOD OF MITERING SIDE AND HEAD JAMBS*

on top of the threshold, and the entire frame is frequently built in the joiner shop and set in place as a unit.

Jambs and thresholds must be well fastened with either large galvanized nails, or screws, with their heads set in counterbores, which are later plugged.

The depth of rabbet for outside doors should be about ⅝ inch. That for inside doors may be ½ inch. The face of the rabbets should be given a slope to allow for the swing out of the inner corner of the door when it is opened.

Thresholds are commonly covered with either sheet brass, or lead, to protect them from chafing.

Former practice has been to fit drop sash in the upper houses of steamers, of the type shown in Figs. 185 and 186. However since this type of sash cannot be made storm tight, and has to be fitted to drop into lead pockets, which are not only troublesome to build, but often give trouble through leaking after the ship is in commission, the type of sash shown in Fig. 188 has been devised, and has recently come into general use. In this type the frame can be built complete in the shop and set in the ship as a unit.

All sash that drop, should be fitted with catches to hold them in any position. In addition they should be fitted with good locks holding them shut, and which cannot be worked from the outside. On sash of Type II, Fig. 188, an ordinary sash lock may be fitted to the parting rail.

All sash and doors, and frames for them, where made in the shop, must be carefully built to the proper bevel to fit the opening on the ship. Very few of these openings, if any, will be perfectly square.

In setting the glass in the sash it is customary to tack a small molding, or bead, against the glass to hold it in place, instead of puttying it in as is done with the sash in buildings. The glass is first set in a rather stiff white lead putty to make it watertight. The bead may either be located on the inside of the sash as shown in Fig. 185, or on the outside as shown in Fig. 188. If set on the inside

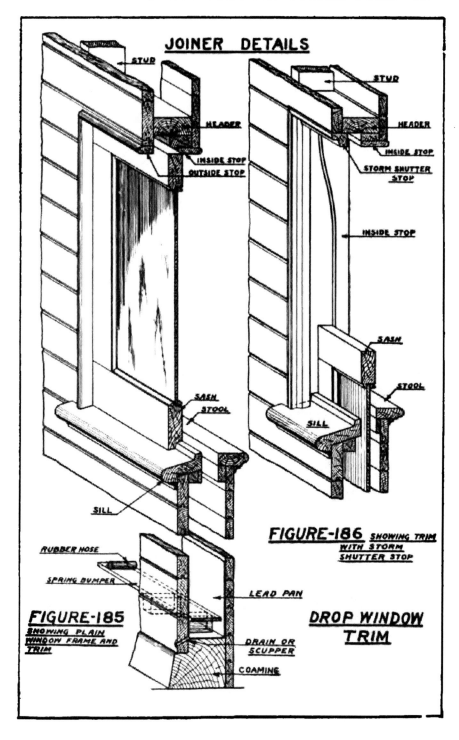

JOINER DETAILS

STUD

HEADER

INSIDE STOP

OUTSIDE STOP

SASH

STOOL

SILL

STUD

HEADER

INSIDE STOP

STORM SHUTTER STOP

INSIDE STOP

SASH

STOOL

SILL

FIGURE-186 SHOWING TRIM WITH STORM SHUTTER STOP

RUBBER HOSE

SPRING BUMPER

LEAD PAN

FIGURE-185 SHOWING PLAIN WINDOW FRAME AND TRIM

DROP WINDOW TRIM

DRAIN OR SCUPPER

COAMING

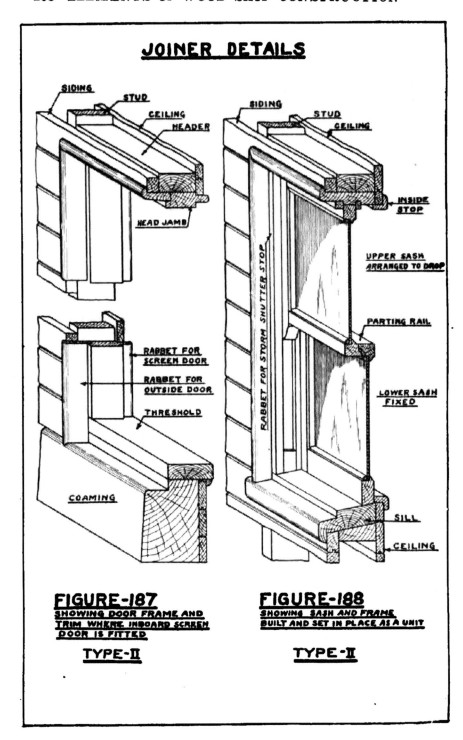

JOINER DETAILS

FIGURE-187
SHOWING DOOR FRAME AND
TRIM WHERE INBOARD SCREEN
DOOR IS FITTED

TYPE-II

FIGURE-188
SHOWING SASH AND FRAME
BUILT AND SET IN PLACE AS A UNIT

TYPE-II

extreme care must be taken in leading, or puttying the glass in to make it watertight. It is generally considered the best practice to place the bead on the outside.

Sash may be used only in houses that are high enough above the water line to be comparatively free from the danger of impact from solid water during storms. In the lower house, such as the poop house, and bridge-deck house, port lights are generally used. They are built of very heavy glass, usually about ¾ inch thick, set in a composition or galvanized iron frame, and are so arranged that they can be made perfectly watertight. In addition, where these ports are fitted to the hull they have storm shutters of metal which would maintain the watertightness of the port even if the glass were broken.

Storm shutters are also fitted to sash openings where they are in any way likely to be exposed to the direct force of a storm. They consist of solid built up heavy wood panels, with a small fixed glass, usually round, set in much the same manner as glass in sash are set.

Various details of trim that may be used in merchant vessels are shown in Figs. 189 to 193 inclusive. The exact form of the details to be used depends largely upon the arrangement of the houses. Also the form of the moldings selected by the designer may be quite different from those shown in the figures, but as a whole, the arrangement of these moldings, and parts, shown here, is quite generally used and gives a house of pleasing appearance though simple in construction as would generally be required on merchant vessels.

Carlines unless quite heavy, are generally sprung to the camber. In wheel and pilot houses, where there are no intermediate supports for the carlines they must be sawn to the full camber. Very often the amount of camber given the house carlines, particularly those in houses not having much thwartship breadth, is greater than the corresponding amount of camber in the deck below. This is done to avoid the appearance of flatness in narrow decks above wider decks, when they are given the same camber.

14

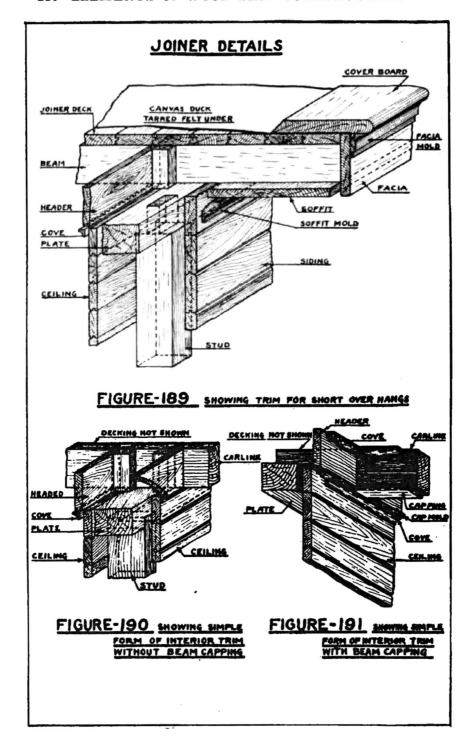

JOINER DETAILS

FIGURE-189 SHOWING TRIM FOR SHORT OVER HANGS

FIGURE-190 SHOWING SIMPLE FORM OF INTERIOR TRIM WITHOUT BEAM CAPPING

FIGURE-191 SHOWING SIMPLE FORM OF INTERIOR TRIM WITH BEAM CAPPING

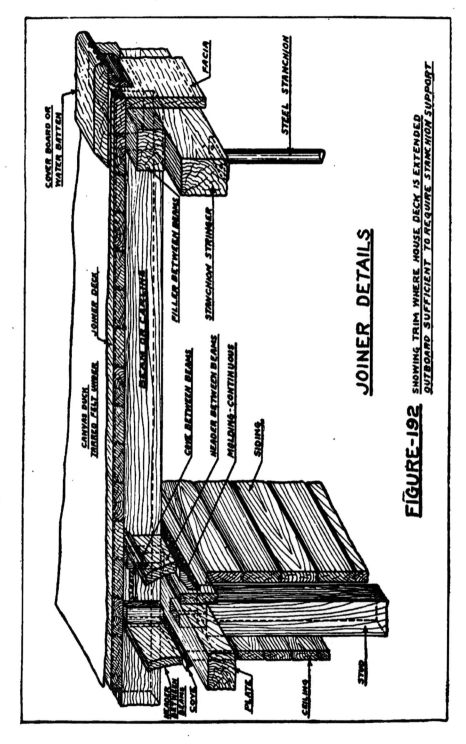

COVER BOARD OR
WATER BATTEN

FACIA

STEEL STANCHION

CANVAS DUCK
TARRED FELT UNDER

JOINER DECK

BEAMS OR CARLINS

FILLER BETWEEN BEAMS

STANCHION STRINGER

COVE BETWEEN BEAMS

HEADER BETWEEN BEAMS

MOLDING-CONTINUOUS

SIDING

HOUSE SIDE
SCYE

PLATE

CEILING

STEP

JOINER DETAILS

FIGURE-192   SHOWING TRIM WHERE HOUSE DECK IS EXTENDED
OUTBOARD SUFFICIENT TO REQUIRE STANCHION SUPPORT

All carlines should be thoroughly fastened at the plates over outside walls, and at the stanchion stringers, where there is wide overhang, with carriage bolts of suitable size. The fastening of finish joiner work in general consists of common nails, finish or casing nails, screws, etc., all of which should be galvanized, or composition. In the pilot house, within a radius of usually not less than four feet from the compass, nothing but copper, or composition fastening is used. It is also customary to make all of the holding down rods for this house of composition.

All joiner hardware, must without exception be solid composition. All door hardware, sash hardware, coat and hat hooks, drawer and wardrobe locks, etc., are therefore of special design for marine purposes.

Interior built in fittings, such as berths, wardrobes, buffets, tables, settees, chart tables, wall desks, etc., are now generally built in the shop, or mill, and when the house structure is completed it is only necessary to scribe them to place. Very often, of course, when such items as lockers, wardrobes, and settees are built up of ceiling, instead of paneling, it may be found best to build them directly in place.

In former times it was not unusual for ship's houses to be built with no plans except those giving a general layout of the rooms, etc. Detail joiner plans were entirely lacking, this matter being left to the head joiner, who arranged the work as in his judgment seemed best. Naturally this required experienced joiners with years of experience, who were at that time available, owing to the small amount of ship work then under way. Today, with a great amount of ship construction under way, experienced joiners are not available in sufficient numbers to permit such a procedure, hence it is now customary to furnish full and complete detail plans of all joiner work, showing its exact form and arrangement in every part. A close study of the figures shown in this chapter, even though much of necessity is omitted, will assist the reader materially in the proper interpretation of these plans.

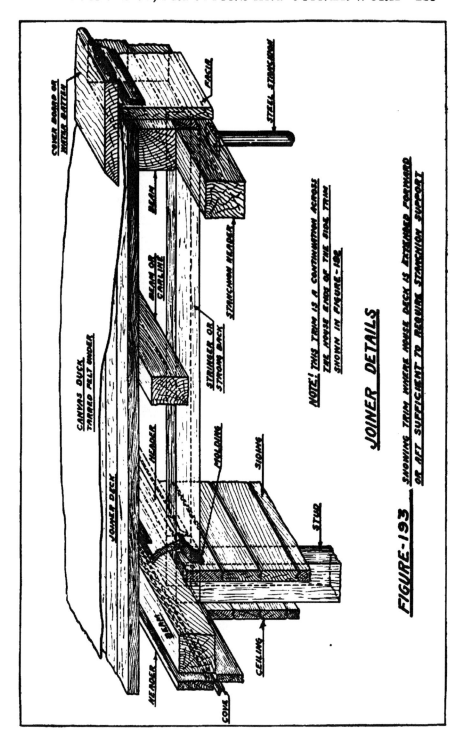

FIGURE-193 — *SHOWING TRIM WHERE HOUSE BACK IS EXTENDED FORWARD OR AFT SUFFICIENT TO REQUIRE STANCHION SUPPORT*

JOINER DETAILS

NOTE. THIS TRIM IS A CONTINUATION ACROSS THE HOUSE ENDS OF THE SIDE TRIM SHOWN IN FIGURE-192.

ADDENDA

In the foregoing discussions, the ship has been considered part by part, and no details have been shown giving the direct relation of one part to another, except those which are directly related to each other. To aid the reader in making direct comparisons between the parts shown and the ship as a whole, Figs. 194 and 195 have been added, showing skeleton inboard profiles of two types of ships that have been discussed. Also, for the same reason, midship sections, of two types of both light and heavy scantling ships are shown in Figs. 195 to 199 inclusive.

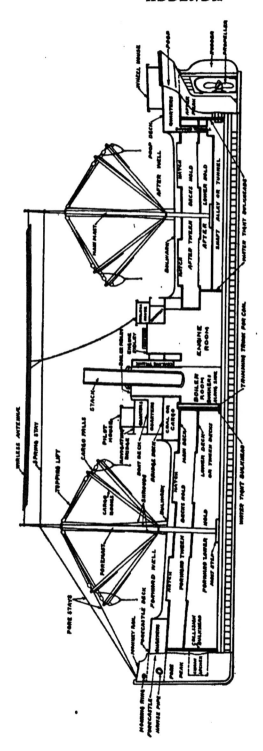

WELL DECK VESSEL
ALSO CALLED
THREE ISLAND TYPE

FIGURE-194

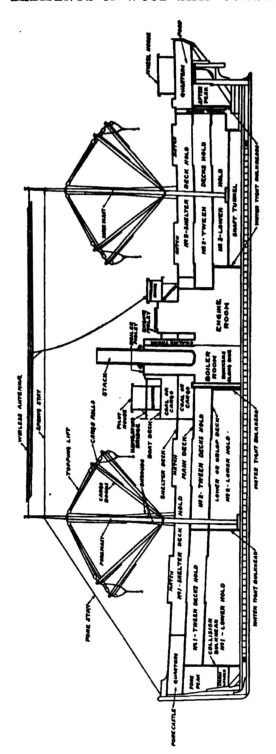

SHELTER DECK VESSEL

FIGURE-195

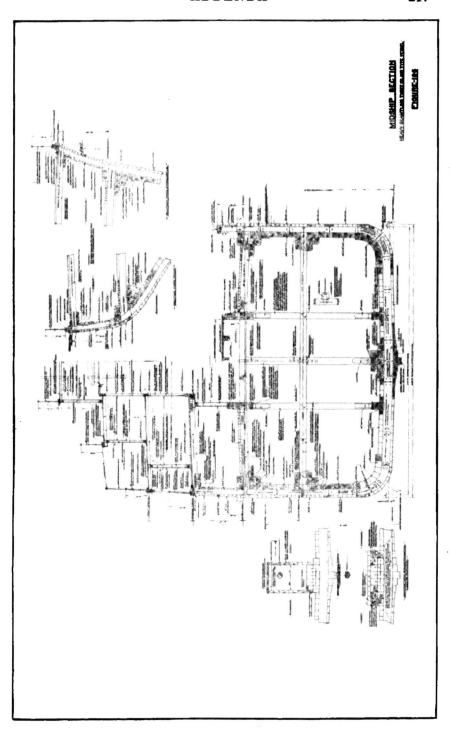

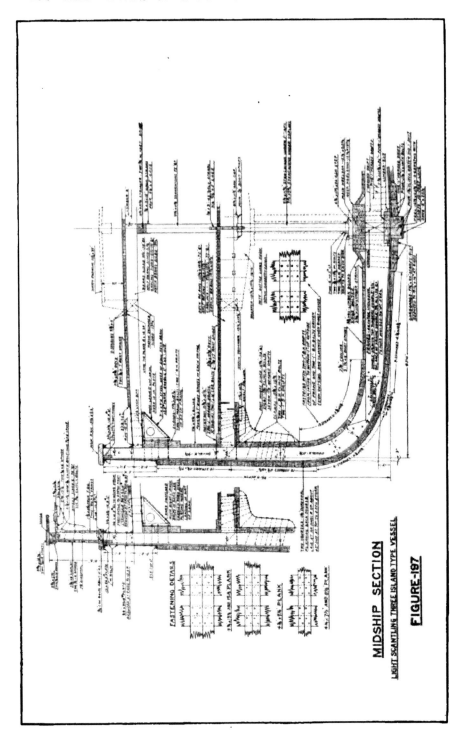

MIDSHIP SECTION

LIGHT SCANTLING THREE ISLAND TYPE VESSEL

FIGURE-197

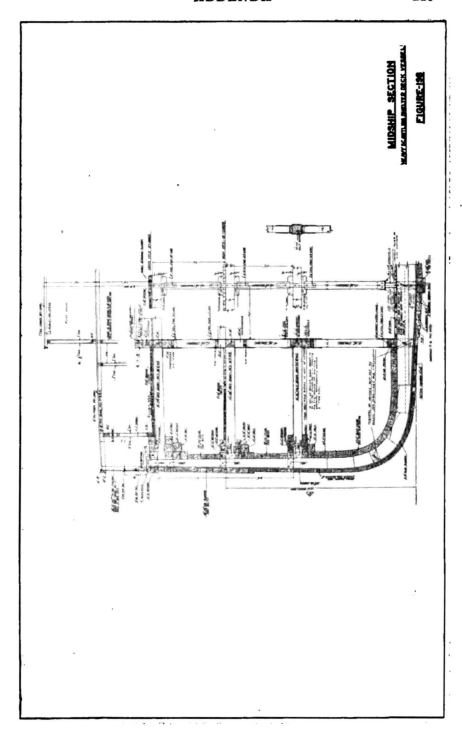

MIDSHIP SECTION
HEAVY HATCH RIB SHELTER DECK VESSEL

FIGURE-53

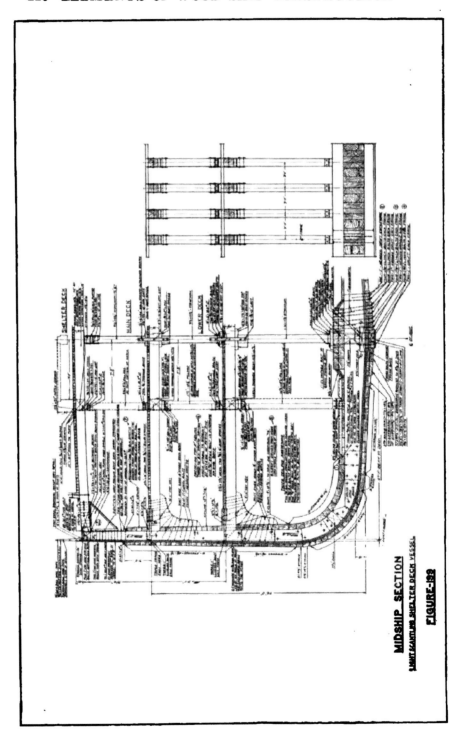

MIDSHIP SECTION

WOOD PLANKING SHELTER DECK VESSEL

FIGURE-122

GENERAL INDEX

221

CPSIA information can be obtained at www.ICGtesting.com
Printed in the USA
LVOW110602261212

313191LV00004B/266/P